Bodysculpture
Plus

Also by Ralph and Valerie Carnes:

Bodysculpture
Bodypower
Sportspower

Bodysculpture Plus

The Aerobic/Resistance Bodyshaping System for Women

Valerie and Ralph Carnes

St. Martin's Press | New York

Photography by Ralph Carnes

BODYSCULPTURE PLUS.
Copyright © 1985 by Valerie Carnes and Ralph Carnes. All rights reserved. Printed in the United States of America. No part of this book may be used or reproduced in any manner whatsoever without written permission except in the case of brief quotations embodied in critical articles or reviews. For information, address St. Martin's Press, 175 Fifth Avenue, New York, N.Y. 10010.

Library of Congress Cataloging in Publication Data

Carnes, Valerie.
    Bodysculpture plus.

      1. Physical fitness for women. 2. Exercise
for women.   3. Weight lifting. 4. Aerobic
exercises.   I. Carnes, Ralph L. II. Title.
GV482.C37 1985   613.7'045   85-1834
ISBN 0–312–08739–X (pbk.)

First Edition
10 9 8 7 6 5 4 3 2 1

To Phyllis and Don, and to Roberta:

*three members of E. M. Forster's
"aristocracy of the sensitive,
the considerate, and the plucky."*

Contents

Acknowledgments

Special thanks are in order to Al Phillips, President of the Chicago Health Clubs, for the use of the superb Marina City CHC facilities as a setting for most of the photographs featuring exercise machines.

Thanks also to the beautiful Nina Nicolai (who was voted top aerobics instructor in Chicago by *Crain's Chicago Business* newspaper) and Staara (Chicago fashion designer and owner of the Staara boutique), who are an inspiration to every woman who sees them work out.

Cheers for Charles Ifergan Studios, Chicago, for the professional work of David and Elham in doing Valerie's hair styling and makeup.

And finally, our sincere thanks to the Church of the Ascension, particular to Rector Edwin A. Norris, Jr., and his assistant, Chuck Kelley, for the use of St. Michael's Hall, where all of the free-weight photographs were shot.

Introduction

When the original *Bodysculpture: Weight Training for Women* was published in 1979, relatively few women had ever dreamed of working out with free weights (barbells and dumbbells) to shape their bodies and lose fat. *Bodysculpture* pioneered weight training as a bodyshaper for women and made it possible for them to enjoy the benefits of an exercise method that, until then, had been almost exclusively male territory.

At the time, we were unaware that we were starting a revolution in exercise for women. But revolution it was, and during the years that followed, women all over America bought barbell and dumbbell sets, built racks and benches, trained with weights, and, to their delight, discovered that here was a system that really worked: it took off pounds, sculpted the body, and made them strong in the bargain.

What's more, at the same time that weight training for women began to take hold, a new type of American woman began to emerge: vital, beautiful, lean, strong, and physically independent. Women of all ages found that they too could look fresh and young by spending just a few hours a week working out in the weight room.

Health clubs caught on quickly and began to introduce exercise machines into women's gyms (and exercise machines are simply a mechanical means of lifting weights). The results were dramatic. In 1978 there were only 2,000 health clubs in the United States. By 1981 there were 54,000. More than 75 percent of the members of these clubs are women.

It's given us tremendous satisfaction over the years to walk into gyms and see women doing the exercises we described in *Bodysculpture*. And it's given us even more satisfaction to see them working out in the men's side of the gym, pumping iron with free weights and enjoying the full benefits of their health-club membership fees. But the greatest satisfaction has come from the hundreds of letters, as well as conversations with women all over America who bought the book, did the exercises, lost weight and kept it off, and reshaped their bodies into the new, young, vital look they wanted. There is a sense of comradeship and mutual concern between us that is its own reward.

Now it's time to take the next step. Along with weight training for women, other kinds of exercise routines have emerged as women have begun to enjoy the freedom that comes with physical activity and regular exercise: aerobic dancing, running, jogging, and Yoga routines for flexibility and gracefulness. Each kind of program makes its own unique addition to the way you look and feel. Brought together into one systematic, easy-to-do program, they offer faster progress than any one of them could offer separately.

And that's where *Bodysculpture Plus* comes in. We've picked up where *Bodysculpture* left off, and we've developed a systematic combination of aerobic, flexibility, and weight-training routines that will enable you to accomplish the following in each workout:

Bodyshaping
Flexibility and gracefulness
Power
Speed and agility

This means faster fat loss, quicker and more effective bodyshaping, gains in strength without loss of agility and speed, and an overall youthful gracefulness that would be impossible if you followed only weight training, only aerobics, or only flexibility routines.

We've worked out specific routines for the most common figure problems. We've developed aerobic and flexibility routines to be done in conjunction with weight training. And we've added a special section on women's bodybuilding, with hints on posing, diet, and contest training. We've also updated one of the most popular features of the first book: the story of Valerie's "Fight with the Fat Demon."

So let's get going! You aren't going to re-create yourself by sitting around reading celebrity beauty books. You've got to get out there and put out the effort. And with the *Bodysculpture Plus* program, the effort will pay off quickly, effectively, and beautifully.

Good luck—write us and tell us about your progress.

Valerie and Ralph Carnes
Chicago, 1984

Bodysculpture Plus

Chapter 1

The *Bodysculpture Plus* Program: What It Is and What It Can Do for You

Bodysculpture: How It All Began

During the mid-seventies, three times a week, Valerie Carnes dragged her husband's old York barbell set out from under the bed and went through a 45-minute weight-training routine. She worked out every other day and performed a variety of weight-training exercises. She and Ralph did the same routine, the same number of repetitions, and the same number of sets. Only the poundages were different.

The results were astonishing, as the photographs on pages 21, 23, and 32 demonstrate. The fat burned off, and Valerie's lifelong water-retention problem cleared up for good. Swollen ankles became a thing of the past, along with tent-size dresses, stretch pants, and all the other fat-hiding clothes she had in her wardrobe.

Exactly as Dr. Barbara Edelstein would describe six years later in her book *The Woman Doctor's Diet for Women,* Valerie first lost weight in her face, then in her upper torso and arms, then in the lower torso and legs. In one year she lost 14 inches from her hips, 7 inches from each thigh, and 5 inches from each ankle, achieving a total weight loss of 75 pounds.

Her weight gradually redistributed itself, and within 16 months the gauntness in her face had been replaced by a vital, youthful sunniness. She had become strong, active, and literally light on her feet. It was a metamorphosis that gave her a new body and a new life.

In 1979 we wrote *Bodysculpture: Weight Training for Women* as a means of bringing this new bodyshaping method to every woman who wanted to look better, feel better, and become the person she had always wanted to be. It worked for Valerie, and she was neither an athlete nor a "natural" beauty.

The book was an instant success. It was the fastest-selling book in Simon and Schuster's 1979 spring line. We made the obligatory book promotion tour, and for the first time in her life Valerie was able to appear in a leotard in public without being ashamed of the way she looked. We even did a 26-week television series on exercises for women for hostess Marijane Vandiver's "Houston Calendar" show on KTRK in Houston, Texas. Eventually we became consultants to the Sports Fitness Institute in Chicago, where we created a women's program based on the book.

We were sitting in a restaurant one day talking about the women's program with the institute's president, Dr. Miles Pohunek, when a slender young woman came up to our table, looked at Valerie, and asked if she was Valerie Carnes. It turned out that she had bought a copy of *Bodysculpture* a year earlier and had lost 85 pounds following the program. The young lady was a physical education instructor in one of Chicago's suburbs. Then came the real surprise: following her own success, the young lady had formed an exercise group at the Aurora, Illinois YMCA, and over a period of six months the women in the group had lost an average of 11 percent body fat by following the *Bodysculpture* program.

A few weeks later we visited the Aurora YMCA and were astonished to find more than 30 energetic women, all of whom had reshaped their bodies with the *Bodysculpture* program. Valerie made a speech, autographed some books, and was moved to tears by the fact that other women who had fought the "Fat Demon" all their lives were winning the fight, thanks to the work she had done.

We've had other experiences—hundreds of them over the past five years—most of which have been different versions of the Aurora story. And one of the greatest things has been seeing women at health clubs all across the country working out with weights, unencumbered by the myths that used to keep women away from barbells as a solution to their weight problems.

One of the funniest experiences happened in Houston one day. Valerie was experimenting with a new way of doing a hip workout described in *Bodysculpture* as the "X-Rated Hip Exercise." A young girl came over and scolded her for not doing it "correctly" and quoted the name we had given the exercise in the book. She never recognized Valerie.

We suppose the funniest experience we had was when we first started working out at the Marina City Chicago Health Club. This was before women were allowed to work out in the men's side of the gym (where the only free weights were located). An irate male club member complained to the management when Valerie started loading up the Olympic bar on the squat racks. He was even more agitated when he discovered that she used about 150 pounds more weight than he did in the lift.

When the paperback edition of *Bodysculpture* was published by St. Martin's Press in 1981, the book climbed right back up the charts and was chosen by *Parade* magazine as a selection for its reader service. You've probably seen it advertised in the Sunday edition of your local newspaper.

Along the way we've tried to figure out exactly why the book has been so popular. We've received bushels of letters and countless telephone calls over the past five years, not to mention the conversations we've had with literally hundreds of women with whom we've compared notes and for whom we've developed personal programs. From what our readers have told us, the following reasons seem most important:

It works. It really works. If you follow the programs recommended in the book, do the exercises properly, and stay on a reasonable diet, you'll lose weight and reshape your body.

The program is easy to understand and simple to do. There's nothing really complicated about it at all. You don't have to be an athlete to do it (Valerie certainly wasn't—she was too fat and clumsy even to survive ballet class in high school).

You don't have to join a health club to do the program. The program can be done at home with simple, inexpensive equipment.

The book tells a true story about a real person. It's not a ghostwritten Hollywood celebrity book trying to cash in on the latest women's market but a real story about a real person who had a real weight problem and wanted to share the solution she found with other real persons who have the same problem.

That's what our readers have told us. It makes sense to us, too. Valerie reshaped her body in our two-bedroom apartment using a 25-year-old barbell set. You can do the same thing.

Now to the new book, the new methods, and the new you. There have been many discoveries during the past five years, and we've been right in the middle of them. We want to share what we've learned both with new readers and with our friends who already know Valerie through the first book.

We've developed ways to combine the *Bodysculpture* programs with other forms of exercise that will assure gracefulness and agility as well as bodyshaping and strength, endurance and speed as well as power and stability. So let's get started with an explanation of how it all works.

Bodysculpture Plus: What It Is and Why It Works

The original *Bodysculpture* program consisted of two kinds of activities: stretching exercises based on karate conditioning routines and weight training based on proven methods of training. The program was a fat-burner and a bodyshaper for several reasons:

1. The workout was a systematic, intensive routine that drastically increased circulation throughout the body and especially in the areas being worked (this is usually called a pump).
2. In doing the exercises, sufficient effort was required to burn calories—and if a reasonable diet was maintained, to burn fat.
3. Overall muscle tone was improved, and that in turn improved posture and carriage.
4. Atrophied or underdeveloped muscles were developed so that the natural contours found in a youthful body were enhanced.

As we said over and over again in *Bodysculpture,* there is nothing magical or mysterious about any of this. Working out burns energy whether it comes from the food you have eaten or from the fat you've stored. If you are burning more energy than you are storing, you'll lose weight.

What was new about the *Bodysculpture* program was the use of weight training for women to accomplish weight-loss goals. It was amusing when people told us that weightlifting was not an aerobic exercise and therefore could not be used to burn fat. Let us tell you why we were so amused.

In the first place, there is a difference between "weight training" and "weightlifting." Weightlifting is not a form of exercise but a sport in which contestants try to lift as much weight as possible in a few carefully prescribed lifts. Each lift takes only a second to perform, so there's not much chance of getting your pulse rate up high enough to burn any fat. Weight training, on the other hand, is not a sport but a systematic form of exercise in which each muscle group in the body is subjected to an intensive workout over a period of time. Weight training is also called "resistance" exercise, because your muscles are fighting the resistance of the weight to be moved.

According to the books on aerobic exercise, the "aerobic effect" is accomplished when your heart reaches a "target pulse rate" (which is computed on the basis of age and general body condition). Running or jogging is usually the preferred type of aerobic exercise since it helps you to reach the target rate quickly and stay there.

Well, all you have to do to make weight training aerobic is use light weights and cut down on the rest intervals between the exercise. This is precisely what you accomplish when you do "circuits" on the exercise machines at health clubs (move from machine to machine without resting between exercises). That's why the circuits work so well in helping you to lose weight.

What *Bodysculpture Plus* Does That the Other Workouts Don't

There is no doubt that running, jogging, cycling, and a host of other exercises will help you to lose weight, as long as you're burning more calories than you're taking in. Furthermore, as many sportsmedicine professionals have pointed out, you don't lose weight *only* when you're exercising. You'll continue to burn calories up to 6 hours *after* your workout is finished, depending on how hard you worked out.

So why is weight training—especially the *Bodysculpture Plus* program—superior to running, jogging, or other forms of aerobic exercise? Let us answer this question with an anecdote that you'll chuckle over. In the summer of 1981 we were invited to participate in a "Sports Expo" at one of the exhibition halls here in Chicago. At the time we were writing the *Hydra-Fitness Exercise Machine User Manual* with Dr. Raymond Manz of Ontario, Canada. Hydra-Fitness machines, through the use of adjustable hydraulic cylinders for resistance, give you both an aerobic and a resistance workout at the same time. In short, you can train for both strength and cardiovascular conditioning at the same time and with the same movements.

One of the local aerobic dancing studios was also represented at the Expo, and young women from the studio put on a show every hour on the main stage. They would dance like mad for 20 minutes at a stretch, and everybody marveled at their stamina.

We were talking to the group leader after one of their shows, and the subject of strength and power training came up. They didn't know what we were talking about. We suggested that doing aerobics alone was just as bad as doing strength training alone. Aerobic training to the exclusion of strength training leaves you with a lot of endurance but no real power. Strength training in isolation leaves you with lots of power but no endurance.

The women didn't believe us. We suggested that they try doing a strength routine during their next show. We borrowed four of the Hydra-Fitness machines, put them on the main stage, and got the women to go through a very *light* resistance workout in which they spent only one minute on each machine.

The best-conditioned woman in the group lasted exactly 6 minutes before we had to help her out of one of the machines and over to a chair. They were all astonished and embarrassed. Remember that the least trained of these women could do aerobic dancing like crazy for over 20 minutes without stopping.

When we were consultants for the Sports Fitness Institute, we saw marathon runners who couldn't jump two feet off the floor. We also saw champion powerlifters who couldn't have run across the street without falling exhausted to the pavement. Which brings us to the point: training is "specific." You get precisely the ability, conditioning, and effect for which you train. If you want endurance without strength, run, jog, or do aerobic dancing. If you want to develop strength or power, use heavy weights and put maximum effort into short workouts. If you want to develop flexibility and gracefulness, forget aerobics and strength training, and stick to Yoga or Tai Chi.

But if you want all of these things *plus* bodyshaping, then the *Bodysculpture Plus* program will give it to you. It is an aerobic/resistance program that combines strength, power, endurance, and flexibility training into a systematic, easy-to-follow routine that will meet all of your beauty and fitness requirements.

A tall order? As in the original *Bodysculpture* program, Valerie herself is proof of the system. As you can see from the photographs throughout the book, she's slender, graceful, and not at all muscular in the way that some women bodybuilders are (more about them later in the chapter on programs). She has never deliberately trained for strength but has instead always done a total-body workout with moderately heavy weights, placing the emphasis on good health and good looks.

Strength and power? Valerie regularly does 10 to 15 repetitions with 275 pounds in the bench squat and 8 to 12 repetitions in the bench press with her body weight. Stamina and endurance? Three times a week she does a workout of 12 exercises for an hour and 10 minutes (with 4 sets per exercise), with no rest between the sets; and she regularly runs from 3 to 7 miles every other day.

Take another look at the photos. Don't worry, her friends who have never worked out with her have trouble believing it, too. Drop by the Marina City Chicago Health Club sometime at 7:30 on a Monday, Wednesday, or Friday morning and work out with us. Seeing is believing!

How Much Time Does the *Bodysculpture Plus* Program Take?

Not as much as you think!

Many of our readers are astonished at the small amount of time it takes to do all the exercises needed to get the results they want. Whenever we talk to working women as well as homemakers, however, the same question is always asked: "How do I find enough hours in the day to keep up a regular exercise program?"

The answer, of course, is that the program doesn't really take much time. Let's do a little elementary school arithmetic, and you'll see what we mean. Here's a typical day at the gym. It'll sound like a full day, but you'll be surprised when you add up the numbers.

Every Monday, Wednesday, and Friday we get up early, drink a glass of orange juice, and head for the Marina City Chicago Health Club. We usually find a parking space at around 7:15 A.M., and by 7:30 we're in the club starting our workout.

The 6:30 crowd is just winding up their workout. Carmelita is finishing her last set of bent-arm pullovers, and Wanda is already in the shower. Around 7:45, Nina and Staara arrive, fantastically dressed and terrifically motivated, and start their daily leg blitz. Rhoda is finishing her 36th lap around the track. Myron begins his circuit through the Nautilus machines; Reggie is busily grinding out heavy rowing; Arnie is popping his biceps with free weight curls; Carl is doing the umpteenth rep of shoulder exercises; Eddie, George, and Doug are spurring each other on to do heavier poundages on the bench press.

It's "leg day" for us, and by 8:00 Valerie is loading up the squat rack with 325 pounds for her fourth set of a pyramid that began with 15 reps with 145 pounds and will end with 3 reps with 325 pounds (she weighs 110 pounds).

We're on the stationary bicycles by 8:15. Then a shower, a quick trip to feed the parking meter, and on to the coffee shop for a glass of juice and the morning newspaper. By 9:00 we've finished our workout, caught up on the news, completed the crossword and the Jumble, and are headed to the office to launch the latest writing project.

On Tuesdays and Thursdays Valerie runs 3 to 5 miles before waking Ralph for a trip to the Rusty Bucket for some scrambled eggs, decaffeinated coffee, the crossword, the Jumble, and a few lists of things to do scrawled on napkins. By 9:30 A.M. we're busy writing at our IBM PC.

Sounds like a lot? Not at all. Our total workout program takes about an hour and a half on Mondays, Wednesdays, and Fridays (including showers and getting dressed), and about an hour for running on Tuesdays, Thursdays, and Saturdays. That's 7½ hours a week, all of them before 9:30 in the morning.

There are 168 hours in the week. You sleep about 56 of them. If you hold a full-time job, you spend 8 hours a day there plus an hour going back and forth, making a total of 63 hours. Sleep and work amount to 119 hours. One hundred and sixty-eight minus 119 is 49. Forty-nine hours a week and you can't use 7½ of them to work out? No wonder you're having problems keeping your weight down!

Think about this, too. If you eat 3 meals a day, you spend at least 2 hours a day, 7 days a week, eating. That's 14 hours a week—more than two times the hours you need for all the workouts that would get you into shape.

Equipment You Need for the *Bodysculpture Plus* Program

One of the beauties of aerobic resistance training is that you can do all the exercises you need to do in the privacy of your own home, with equipment that is surprisingly inexpensive. However, if you belong to a health club or want to join one in order to get the reinforcement provided by working out with a group, you can do your *Bodysculpture Plus* program there, too.

But first, let's talk about what you need to do your workouts at home. Here's a list of the basic equipment, which can be purchased at almost any sporting goods store, at department stores, or at large stores, such as Sears or Montgomery Ward.

Item	Description
Barbell Bar	A chrome or iron bar about 5 feet long with collars that fasten at each end to hold the plates
Barbell Plates	Disk-shaped weights made either of iron or vinyl-coated cement to fit onto the barbell
Dumbbell Set	Two small bars (about a foot long) with collars to hold the plates
Bench	A sturdy bench (a picnic table bench will do) narrow enough to allow your arms to drop below the level of your body when you do bench presses (see photograph page 124)

Cost: less than $50

That's the basic outfit. Below are a few items you may want to add if you're thinking about building a home gym.

Item	Description
Bench-Press Bench	A narrow bench with a rack to hold the barbell until you lift it off and do the exercise
Squat Rack	A rack (made of metal or wood) to hold the barbell until you lift it off and do the exercise

Cost: from around $35 to $250 for the bench-press bench; around $40 to $250 for the squat rack

And if you really want to go first class and have the extra room to put the equipment, you may want to look into the following items:

Item	Description
Dumbbell Racks	Racks for the dumbbells to keep them off the floor
Multiple Dumbbells	A set of dumbbells with fixed weight values (for example, pairs of 15-, 20-, 25-, and 30-pound dumbbells) so you don't have to change weights during a workout
Olympic Barbells	These barbells are designed especially with Olympic weightlifting or power lifting in mind. If you are building a family gym, you may want to invest the money in an Olympic set for your ambitious teenagers. York is the standard manufacturer in the field.
Power Racks	These are all-purpose metal racks that allow you to use really heavy weights in the squat, the press, and the bench press without having someone "spot" you while you're doing the exercise.
Exercise Machines	Our best recommendation for home gym exercise machines is the Hydra-Fitness line. Because they use adjustable hydraulic cylinders instead of iron plates, the machines are light in weight, practically noiseless, clean, and essentially maintenance-free. We have a multiple-station Hydra-Fitness machine sitting right here in our living room (it's about the size of a reclining chair). The machine was originally designed to give the crewmen on nuclear submarines a total body workout. It has a bench press/rowing station, a leg extension/leg curl station, and a shoulder press/pulldown station. Although the machine was designed specifically for these 6 exercises, we've developed 22

Item	Description
	additional exercises you can do on it. There are many lightweight machines on the market, but this one is by far the best.

Costs: Dumbbell racks range from $75 to $250. Multiple dumbbells range from $25 apiece for painted iron or vinyl sets to $150 apiece for fancy chrome. Olympic and power-lifting barbell sets start at around $360 for a York Olympic Standard bar and 300 pounds of plates.

Power racks range from around $150 to $600. The Hydra-Fitness Total Power multiple exercise machine costs (as of February 1984) $2,500 plus shipping from Belton, Texas. Separate pieces of equipment run at a fraction of the cost of the multiple unit.

If you've never bought exercise equipment before, here are a few tips on how to get your money's worth. Let's talk about free weights first:

1. If you buy a set made of iron, check the plates for ragged, protruding metal along the edges and sides. If the plates were manufactured in a hurry, the metalworker may have forgotten to grind off the rough edges, and you can get a cut finger if you don't watch out.
2. If you live in an apartment or condominium, you should buy a set with plates made of cement-filled vinyl. They're quieter when you set them down, and they don't mar the floors or the rug with rust.
3. Take a look at the collars. The better ones have a permanent little handle on the set screws, so you can tighten them without a hassle. The cheaper ones have set screws, but a small wrench is needed to tighten them. When you're in the middle of a workout, you shouldn't have to look for a wrench. Occasionally, you will find barbell and dumbbell sets with plastic collars. Avoid them. They tend to break when you start using heavier weights.
4. Make sure the benches and racks are sturdy! Remember that they've got to hold you *and* the weights up!
5. Check all vinyl plates for splits along the seams.

6. If you buy an Olympic-style barbell set, check the ends of the bar for excessive play.
7. Don't be overly impressed by chromed equipment. It's far too expensive to make it a good value for a home gym. Further, chromed bars become oily and slippery with use and can slip right out of your hands. The best bars (especially the Olympic-style ones) are made of unchromed steel.
8. Check the barbell bar's knurling (the crisscrossed lines cut into the bar to give your hands a good grip). It should be fairly deep and symmetrically cut. Watch out for poor knurling with sharp edges.
9. Make sure the upholstery on the benches is durable. The best material is industrial Mylar. Remember that perspiration is corrosive to many kinds of simulated leather or cloth.
10. Before you buy anything new, check the classified section of your local newspaper for exercise equipment. You may find some real bargains.

Here are a few tips on the purchase of exercise machines:

1. Again, check the classified section of your daily newspaper. Small health clubs sometimes go out of business, and the exercise machines are often sold for only a fraction of their original cost. You may find equipment made by the leaders in the field going for peanuts.
2. In choosing an exercise machine, remember that you need a machine or set of machines that will give you a total body workout, not just a single-function machine.
3. Remember also that chains and cables will eventually have to be replaced, so count maintenance costs into the total you plan to spend.
4. If you buy one of the weighted system machines such as Nautilus, Universal, or Paramount, the stacks of heavy plates will require that you place the machines either in your basement on the slab or in your garage. An apartment or home floor simply will not support the weight of these machines.
5. If you buy one of the popular machines (such as Soloflex) that use rubber bungee cords to provide the resistance, check on the replacement cost of the bungees before making the purchase.
6. If you want to go first class without spending a fortune, buy Hydra-Fitness exercise machines. They're the only machines on the market that will give you what is called an "omnikinetic" workout, combining strength, power, speed, and aerobics training all in one machine.

Workout Clothes You'll Need for Bodysculpture Plus

The *Bodysculpture Plus* program is probably one of the least expensive programs you'll ever undertake. Once you have the basic equipment—or access to a health club that does—you need very little else besides clothing to get started. Here's what you need to buy for your first time in the gym.

1. A basic warm-up suit, or T-shirt and shorts. These are the two most common outfits women are wearing to the gyms today, and they're both equally acceptable for gym wear. If you're still heavier than you'd like to be, the warm-up suit or a jogging suit is a good choice since it camouflages heavy hips, thighs, and tummy.

   For summer wear, a loose T-shirt and boxer-style running shorts (no high-on-the-thigh cuts until you're in top shape!) are good choices. And that doesn't have to be a dull combination; now that lines like Calvin Klein and Lollipop are bringing out pastel-colored men's-style underwear for women, you have your pick. Layer a tank top and shorts over a pastel leotard, add a pale-colored terry-cloth headband and socks, and you'll look marvelous.

2. As you trim down to the size you want to be, try some of the new leotard styles and shapes. Gone are the days when a single style—scoop neck, long sleeves, low-cut legs—was standard. Now there are tank tops, crisscrossed straps, lace-trimmed styles, diagonal stripes (very slimming, by the way), even dolman-sleeved and blouson tops. The whole leotard market has boomed in the past few years, and you can literally take your pick of hundreds of styles. Try on several different ones before you buy: you will find at least one that is both flattering and comfortable.

3. A lifting belt. If you're going to be handling even light weights, you need a lifting belt to give lower back support in lifts that involve bending, squatting, or overhead lifts. Choose the widest style you can find (a man's size Small will fit even the most petite woman). Make sure that the leather is fairly thick and stiff to afford maximum support for your back. Soft leather may be prettier, but it simply doesn't provide the support you need. Remember that even though a belt may be stiff initially, it will soften as it wears. Cost is about $20–25, and it will last forever.

4. Thin to medium-thin socks and running or lifting shoes. Although we still see many women trying to work out in bare feet or ballet shoes, we recommend running or lifting shoes for the gym. You need shoes that grip the floor for lifts such as the squat and shoulder shrug otherwise you may lose your balance. And for doing leg presses, curls, and extensions, you need shoes to avoid injuring your feet. Make sure you have socks (thin, not thick, to follow the contours of both your feet and your shoes) or put your shoes on directly over footed leotards if you prefer.

5. The extras: wristbands, sweatbands, headbands, leg warmers, thin belts, etc. These are fun, colorful, inexpensive extras that add pizzazz to even the most humdrum looks. Try a pretty pastel headband and wristbands, plus leg warmers, to spark a monochromatic leotard or sweatsuit. They cost only a few dollars each and are now available even in supermarkets and drugstores. And in cold weather, leg warmers provide extra protection against pulled muscles in the injury-prone calf and ankle areas.

6. A well-stocked gym bag. Especially if you're going directly from the gym to work or meetings, you'll want to pack a mini-makeup and hair care center in your bag. A compact-size hot roller set or curling iron, plus a travel-size blow dryer, are essential if you intend to shampoo and dry your hair before work. Scout the stores for sample-size shampoo and rinse bottles, which take up less room in a gym bag than regular sizes.

    You'll also want to carry extra panty hose, covered rubber bands for your hair, Tampax or napkins, a small disposable razor, soap or body shampoo, and perhaps a small first-aid kit and compact sewing kit for emergencies. Add your makeup kit (the dime-store plastic cases with see-through sides are ideal). Valerie always throws in some safety pins and Scotch tape for quick hem repairs. Some women even pack a small travel iron or steamer to smooth out the wrinkles in a dress or suit that's been stuffed into a small locker too long.

    And don't forget a towel, a washcloth or sponge, and a shower cap (if you don't intend to wash your hair). If you need to carry your workout outfit back with you to the office, take along a small plastic bag for your damp workout gear or swimsuit. Once at the office, you can hang the damp togs in a hidden corner or on the coatrack. Valerie hangs her leotard on the pull of a file drawer next to her typewriter.

7. A good running or sports bra. Whether you're large- or small-busted, this is an item you need to buy. Don't think you can work out braless

without experiencing some amount of sag. You can't! Invest in a good sports-style bra (the ones with crisscrossed front supports are especially good). Some sports styles even have hidden money/key pouches for outdoor runners. But don't try to make do with the same minimal style you may wear under your business suits or dresses. Get a support style especially meant for sports, and WEAR it!

Now you know all you need to know in order to make an informed judgment about the clothes and equipment you should buy.

Should You Join a Health Club?

The answer to this question depends on a lot of things, including cost, equipment needs, goals, and personal psychology. Let's talk about what a health club has to offer that working out at home doesn't. Then let's talk about your own personal goals and how much money it will cost to reach them by going the health club route.

The Marina City Chicago Health Club is a fine example of the best type of deluxe club. It's located about six blocks from the heart of downtown Chicago, right on the Chicago river, in the lower level of the Marina City condominium and docking complex. It's convenient for people who work in the Loop area. Parking is plentiful (especially in the morning), and the club is open seven days a week from morning until late at night.

There is a women's gym complete with new Keiser pneumatic exercise machines, programmable stationary bicycles, and plenty of room for aerobic dancing and other types of exercise that involve leaping and moving around. Women also have access to the men's gym, which features a complete line of Nautilus equipment, several Universal machines, a set of squat racks, two bench-press benches, a power rack, an extensive collection of dumbbells, and three Olympic-style barbell sets. Add to these features saunas in both the women's and men's gyms, as well as steam baths, a running track, and a full-size swimming pool and you've got all the gymnasium that anyone could ever want.

Many women would rather work out in a gym than at home because of the social aspects of working out with a group. Each member tends to support the others, and working out becomes a pleasant social outing in addition to being a constructive form of exercise. Furthermore, some people find it much easier to get up, get dressed, and go down to the gym for a workout than to get up, put on a leotard, and go down to the basement or into the spare room to work out. It's part of the psychology of "getting cranked up" in the morning. In addition, many women like the variety of activities available in a gym—swimming, dancing, saunas—all of which enhance the task of working out and make it seem more like fun and less like a chore.

The cost of membership in a good health club varies with location and the number of "extras" such as saunas, etc. In downtown Chicago, you'll pay anywhere from $600 to $1,500 a year, plus renewal fees of from $250 to $600 per year. In smaller cities or in the suburbs, these costs are often halved or quartered.

WHAT TO LOOK FOR WHEN YOU SHOP FOR A HEALTH CLUB MEMBERSHIP

1. The first thing to do if you're really serious about joining a health club is to watch the newspapers for membership specials. They tend to be seasonal (late summer is the "off season," so keep your eyes open for sales), and the savings amount to 50 percent or more.
2. Don't let the salesperson rush you through the club. Take your time and ask a lot of questions. Remember, the salesperson gets a commission for every membership sold. The odds are that you're just another potential sale to this person. Let the sale be made at your pace, not his or hers.
3. Make sure that, as a female member, you have access to all of the equipment in the gym. If you're going to use the gym for your *Bodysculpture Plus* program, it would be a nasty surprise to find out, after you've signed a contract, that women aren't allowed to use the weights or the machines.
4. Since you'll have your copy of *Bodysculpture Plus* you won't need any instruction for free weights and aerobic training. But new exercise machines are being designed even as we write these lines. There may be some machines with which you are unfamiliar. Ask the salesperson about them. If the answers don't make sense in light of what you've read in the book, it may be that you're in a club where sales competence prevails over exercise competence.
5. Excuse yourself for a few minutes and go to the women's room. While you're there, ask the women members what they think about the club. They'll tell you if women aren't treated fairly. And while

you're there, look to see if the club is kept clean—especially the showers.

6. Make sure you can come to the club whenever it's open. Don't buy a membership in a club that restricts you to certain times of the day or days of the week.

7. Some clubs alternate days for women and men. If you plan to work out with your boyfriend or husband, make sure you can both come on the same day and use the same gym.

8. Make sure you'll be left alone to follow your own program. Some gyms regiment the workouts (especially for women) so they can get you in and out in a hurry to make room for the next group. The more groups, the more money, get it?

9. Ask yourself if you really need all the equipment and other benefits of the club. Remember that although you may never use the swimming pool, the sauna, the steam bath, the massage room, the tanning devices, the juice bar, the workout gear boutique, the hot tubs and whirlpools, the racquetball, handball, and tennis courts, your membership fee is helping the club to pay the cost of having all that stuff.

10. Remember the initial fee is literally just the beginning. You'll have to pay a renewal fee every year as long as you continue working out at the club.

11. Remember also that you don't have to belong to a health club to follow your *Bodsculpture Plus* program! You can do everything you have to do to succeed with the program right there at home, without all the expensive equipment, without a lot of skinny people staring at you while you try to peel away the fat you want to lose.

How to Get Started on Your *Bodysculpture Plus* Program

Woody Allen once said that the first thing you have to do if you want to be on television is show up. Same here. If you want to lose fat, trim and slim down, and shape your body to look like all those California girls, you've first got to show up. And that means:

1. Get down to the sporting goods shop and get yourself an inexpensive barbell set and a good pair of running shoes.

2. Read this book and go over the exercises in your mind.
3. Work out a personalized program that suits your particular needs.
4. Get to work on your *Bodysculpture Plus* program!

You'll see a difference in 14 days. Within a month, you'll be taking in your clothes. In 60 days, you'll be shopping for smaller sizes. In 90 days, you'll have a new you (and you'll keep her, too!).

Got it? Let's get to work!

Chapter 2

Whatever Happened to the Fat Demon?

Six years ago I sat down at my typewriter—just as I'm doing today at the word processor—and wrote a story. It was called "The Fight with the Fat Demon," and it told the story of my lifelong struggle with every woman's mortal enemy: the "Fat Demon" that is always lurking just out of sight for even the leanest of us.

The Fat Demon was no stranger to me. I grew up in an era when Twiggy was every teenager's idol and "starved to near perfection" was the look of the day. Models, at least for a time, seemed to grow thinner each time they appeared in the pages of the glossy women's magazines. And in the midst of all that thinness, I was fat.

The original *Bodysculpture* told my story. "In my previous incarnation as a Fat Soul," I wrote, "I was never any competition for Mama Cass. But I was Fat. I had plump arms, a round little protruding tummy, a veritable shelf of a *derrière*, bulging thighs, and piano legs with thick ankles." And I had them from age eleven or twelve until the day that I hauled out the weights and started on the program that would one day be called "the Bodysculpture program."

Whenever I go on tour now I'm always met with the same question: "How much did you weigh at your heaviest?" The answer is, I don't know. Publicly I confess to 185, but about that time I discovered that my trusty scales were actually about 5 pounds light. Depressed at that discovery, I simply quit weighing for a while (if you ignore the problem, maybe it will go away)—so I can't say what my top weight was. Certainly 190, but probably more.

Back to my former career as town Fat Girl. *Bodysculpture* tells the tale: "I was a cuddly baby, an adorably chubby toddler, a plump little girl, a chunky pre-teen, a stocky adolescent, and finally, a self-loathing graduate student who starved herself down to 135 pounds on a balanced diet of black coffee and No-Doz. One year, one marriage, and one Ph.D dissertation later, I ballooned back up to 175 pounds."

Mine, unfortunately, was a classic case of the yo-yo syndrome. From my prepubescent years on, I went up and down the scales in swings of 20 pounds or more. If I literally starved myself on 300 calories a day or less, I could get down to 145 or even 140. If I ate "normally"—even one or two normal meals—I gained wildly, often 8 or 10 pounds over a weekend.

And it wasn't that I wasn't dieting. I dieted all the time. Food to me meant "diet." I drank Slender, Metrecal, diet sodas by the carload, devoured carrot sticks, diet gelatin, and cottage cheese. I weighed my food and washed it like a raccoon. I measured portions in fractions of an ounce. I passed up desserts and pizzas when all my teenage friends were pigging out. But I was still fat.

The real turning point in my fight with the Fat Demon came on a cold, windy Saturday in March in the late seventies. It was one of those clean, brisk early-spring days in Chicago when the air is so clear that if you look across the lake you can see Michigan City, Indiana, from your apartment window.

So I decided to go out shopping in search of a pair of blue jeans. Sounds strange, I know, but at that moment in time I didn't own a single pair of jeans. Everyone else was into those marvelous cat's-eye-blue faded denims, and I decided I had to have a pair. So I arranged to meet Ralph at our favorite sidewalk place on Rush Street—Melvin's—and went off on the famous jeans safari.

Was I in for a shock! I must have tried on 20 pairs of jeans that fateful morning. I tried jeans in budget stores, Magnificent Mile department stores, boutiques that were too *haute* for words, and in friendly, funky little stores where the salespeople had frizzled hair and big smiles and really wanted to help me find what I wanted ("Are those still too small? . . . Oh wow, I don't think we stock anything bigger . . .").

We talk about epiphanies, and I've had my share. But one of the most dramatic realizations of my entire life came in that last funky little shop where I stood in silence, facing the mirror, just me and my too, too solid flesh. There we were, confronting each other across the distance that separates flesh and reflection, and for the first time in my life I said aloud to myself, "Valerie, you are FAT." And then, being a practical soul, my next question to myself was, "So what are you going to do about it?"

Valerie "before" at 175 lbs.

I did two things. I got out of that shop posthaste. I got back into my trusty polyester stretch pants and bolted. I had to get away from my reflection with all its sags, rolls, bags, and protrusions in all the wrong places. And I got out into the street, where I tried to cry and couldn't. I was too angry to cry—angry with myself for having allowed things to reach this point. And frustrated that of all the pairs of jeans in the Windy City, there wasn't one that I could fit into.

Over lunch at Melvin's I picked over my salad and told Ralph the whole miserable story. "Look at all those women in the street wearing jeans," I raged. "Some of them are no smaller than I am. How come they can buy jeans and I can't?"

The truth of the matter was simple: my thighs had blossomed to over 30 inches and with a small frame—only 5'6½"—any jeans that fit over my thighs swallowed up that small frame. I was grossly out of proportion and couldn't admit it.

Ralph, as usual, had an idea. Why not try weight training, he suggested, recalling that as a kid he'd helped himself on the road to recovery from rheumatic fever with a weight-training program. A lifelong devotee of weight training, he'd followed competition weightlifting and bodybuilding in the magazines for years. He'd watched his favorite contestants build up, trim down, get definition, pump up, and literally reshape their bodies by pumping iron. If it worked for them, why not for me?

I had all the stock female responses: "Ha! *Me* lift weights? The very idea! I don't want to turn into the Hulk, I want to be thin. If I lift weights I'll get those big, bulky muscles and I don't want to look like that. I just want to be thin, thin, thin . . ."

Ralph listened patiently to this tirade. But later that afternoon he pulled out a stack of magazines and showed me a few before and after photos of bodybuilders who had been on three- and six-month programs. The difference was startling. Shapeless men with skinny arms, shoulders, thighs, and sagging beer bellies had turned themselves into pretty impressive specimens with tapering V-shaped torsos, tremendous abdominal definition, shapely thighs, and gorgeous backs and arms. Even my untrained eye had to admit that they looked fantastic. For the first time in my life I got the point: the key to reshaping one's body was not starvation, but EXERCISE.

That afternoon I hauled out the barbells (Ralph's old set, now gathering dust in the storage room) and started on a workout routine. At first I worked only my legs—my trouble spot. I did squats (my first one nearly sent me through the floor—Ralph had to pull me up to get me on my feet again). A lifetime of inactivity hadn't exactly equipped me for this.

Despite Ralph's warnings, I overdid it. After I finished that first workout I tried to get up and walk to the elevators to go to the apartment commissary on the first floor. I made it about halfway down the hallway before my knees literally collapsed. I just couldn't make it any farther.

But something in my head and psyche got turned around that day. I had made up my mind that I wasn't going to be fat anymore, no matter what it took to do it. I rearranged my schedule so that I got up an hour earlier each day (me, who had never gotten out of bed more than 30 minutes before time to leave for work). While I watched the early-morning talk shows, I did squats, calf raises, leg curls, and spinal hyperextensions. In the evenings when I came home I did arm, upper body, and hip/waist routines on alternate days.

And the effort paid off. By the end of that first summer of weight training I had shed 9 inches from my hips, 3 from each thigh, and 2 from each calf. My waist was down and my tummy was disappearing—so much so that I went on vacation with my first swimsuit ever, a white bikini that I considered the ultimate in slim chic. Ralph made a picture of me that I copied and hung on the refrigerator door. Several times a day, I stood and looked at it in disbelief. I couldn't believe it was me. And by September I went back to one of the supertrendy boutiques and bought those French designer jeans I had coveted in the spring. My weight was down to under 130 pounds for the first time since I was a teenager, and I was still losing.

Valerie "halfway" at 140 lbs.

By now I was really in the spirit of things. While I continued the waist, hip, and leg routine, I added a short run on alternate days. First an eighth of a mile, huffing and puffing all the way, then a quarter, then a half, and finally a full mile! (Now my daily run is 4 to 7 miles, but we all have to start somewhere.)

And in the midst of this Ralph and I found time to write the prospectus for the book that later became *Bodysculpture* (we started it during a dismal August, sitting in my parents' den, in the midst of a rained-out vacation during which the car broke down and had to be placed in the shop for 10 days). Our newly acquired agent, Dominick Abel, sold it to Simon and Schuster and we began to create a systematic program with the very routines that I had used in my own fight with the Fat Demon.

Now I'm looking back on the whole story from the vantage point of five years afterward, and I realize that not only have I changed tremendously but the world around me has changed, and some of the attitudes and ideas that gave rise to that first book were on the cutting edge of those changes. For one thing, women all over America have changed, perhaps more than any other single group in our society. They're not afraid of being strong and healthy and assertive; they're not afraid of being themselves.

They no longer fear competition, either at work or in the gym. They no longer feel that they have to look a certain way or be arrested at a certain age. Instead of the monolithic sixties standard (everyone had to be superskinny and under 25), there is a new and appealing diversity in images for women. In fact, if you watch the media closely, you'll find that our new Superwoman is not the darling of the idle rich but the involved, intelligent, busy career woman who matches her successes on the job with victories in the gym and on the running track or tennis courts. She works hard and plays hard, sweats with the best of them, enjoys her body, and isn't ashamed to admit it. She doesn't waste time coveting someone else's body; she's chiefly interested in perfecting the one she has.

Let me share with you a few anecdotes that illustrate these changes. When I first started working out with the *Bodysculpture* program, I learned pretty quickly that weight training for women was considered by most normal citizens to be a part of the lunatic fringe. Women weightlifters/bodybuilders were associated with stocky peasant women who spoke in thick accents, wore rubber workout suits, grunted and sweated a lot, and had bulging biceps.

But when I began to change, even my most conservative friends were obviously impressed. My colleagues, startled at the metamorphosis of once-chubby Valerie into this creature with prominent cheekbones and a small waistline, all dropped by the office to chat. When they asked, "What are you dong? Let me in on the secret?" I told them, "Try weight training."

They couldn't have been more shocked if I'd told them I was into vampirism or leather fetishes. They either made some wisecrack about 10-foot Amazons in steel tank tops carrying spears or Olympic weightlifters on steroids. Some of the trendier types mentioned the Hulk or Conan the Barbarian. Most of them simply coughed politely and then bolted from the room, pleading an urgent meeting. Clearly, women pumping iron weren't something you talked about in polite society. Exit Valerie, foot in mouth.

So I learned to live with my shameful, if effective, secret vice. I tucked my beloved barbell plates, collars, and handles out of sight in a big antique-looking copper tub under my desk. Nosy visitors were told that it was full of dirty clothes or old newspapers. The iron bars I hid behind the closet door when dinner guests came. Only my best friends knew that in my secret life, by night, under the full moon, I turned into Valerie the Wondrous Weightlifter.

The lesson was underscored when an old acquaintance came to town to visit. He spent the evening in our favorite Greek restaurant with us, admiring every pretty girl in sight ("Wow, look at the shape on that one!"). But the next morning he awakened, bleary-eyed, to the inspiring sight of Valerie in sweatsuit doing leg presses in the spare room with 150 pounds on the bar.

I thought he would be impressed. He was, but not in quite the right way. As he choked down a cup of coffee and muttered something about my being "compulsive" and "unfeminine," I asked him, "Hey, how do you think I got to look like that girl in the restaurant last night?" He managed to get out something about "natural" good looks and fled from the room. Like many people, both men and women, he liked the *results* of exercise; it was the *means* of getting there that he couldn't handle. Women who ran or lifted weights to get in shape were doing something to cheat Mother Nature, and that was a little too unnatural for this purist.

Throughout the mid- and late seventies many people, women as well as men, continued to be suspicious of heavy exercise for women. Floor exercises, a little light ballet or stretching were okay, but real work-outs—never! The owner of one health club in Houston whom I inter-viewed was asked why the women's gym had no weights over 10 pounds (since I was squatting with over 150 pounds even then, I was a bit curious about this). He actually told me with a straight face, "Oh, women don't need to work out with weights. They just like all the light stuff, all the fluff, so we give 'em a little dance and a little jumping around—stuff like that. They don't need all that heavy iron."

Even after *Bodysculpture* was sold, I still found myself treading on the proverbial thin ice. Our original editor asked us to tone down the advice on nutrition (too much to ask of the readers that they cut out salt, sugar, preservatives, and fat) and photograph the exercises using only light weights. When I went on television shows, I found myself having to adjust to working with 3-pound pink-and-blue dumbbells when I routinely did the same exercises with 20 pounds or more at home—all because TV producers thought that women viewers would be turned off by a strong, agile woman.

Several television producers, in fact, demanded that I use lighter weights for the squat when I worked before the cameras. I also learned that sweating was a no-no, so I made sure to powder over my makeup before I got under the studio lights. The producers and hosts all feared that the sight of someone working out and sweating would turn off the women viewers. Actually, the women loved it. The greatest response we had to our TV miniseries in Houston with our friend Marijane Vandiver came from women who appreciated the fact that I actually did my morning workout right there on camera, doing the sets and reps along with them while Ralph counted for me, and that I worked up an honest sweat while I was doing it.

The funniest response of all came from one of the major women's magazines. I sent them an excerpt of *Bodysculpture* along with some terrific color shots of me demonstrating some Universal exercise equipment—running on a treadmill, etc. The editor wrote back. She was torn about the article. On the one hand she and the staff loved it and even liked the photos, but on the other they felt that the women in their audience (in 1980, no less) weren't quite ready for a story about women and weights.

So the editor came up with a solution. Although she thought the story had merit, she felt that it was just too *avant-garde* for her readers. Couldn't I rewrite the article so that there was no mention of weights? But the whole point of the weight-loss program was that it was done with weights. Weight training had helped me to reshape my body when every other kind of exercise had failed. And this editor wanted me to leave out the weight training and stress the other exercises—the ones that didn't work!

I didn't even have to think it over. I called back and said thanks but no thanks. I wanted badly to get into the magazine, but it was a compromise I just couldn't make. It seemed to me that if I had to lie to get into the magazine, I would be doing a tremendous disservice to the very women who needed help the most. No thanks. No way. And no article about *Bodysculpture*.

I also learned that I always had to look superfeminine when I went on promotional tours. Women always asked the same questions: "Won't it build big muscles?" and "Won't I get stiff and awkward and musclebound?" They were reassured by the sight of me in my lace-trimmed leotard showing photos of clothes I had modeled for a designer friend. Women had been so conditioned by the media and by male athletes to think of weights as forbidden territory that they needed constant reassurance that picking up a barbell would not turn them into Mr. Olympia.

But the eighties began to change all that. Women ceased to be afraid of their own strength. *Esquire* magazine, always on the cutting edge of popular culture movements, published an article on the new woman and extolled the joys of being around strong, competent, well-muscled women. Women bodybuilders became the new sex symbols of the era. Movies such as *Flashdance, Grease,* and *All That Jazz* contributed to our awareness of the beauty of motion. Women began to be admitted to men's gyms, where they could pump iron, puff, pant, groan, sweat, and work along with men. The day of the strong woman had come, and it was a joy to behold.

At about this time another change came about that I also applaud: the superthin craze is over, thank goodness. Women all over the country are growing savvy about diet, body fat, nutrition, and weight. When we started the *Bodysculpture* program in the late seventies, every woman's goal was simply to weigh as little as was humanly possible. ("May God reward you by making you invisible!" said my dear friend Arthur to me by way of blessing as we stumbled out for our morning run at 5:00 A.M. on a steamy Houston day.)

The eighties have brought us a welcome change. Current research on height/weight tables indicates that the tables are, if anything, a bit low for most women of average height and build. We're sophisticated enough to understand that it's not weight but percent body fat that matters. And have you looked lately? Even the fashion models featured in the top women's magazines are lean, not skinny; healthy-looking and vital, not emaciated. Women in gyms and spas across the country have learned to assess themselves and each other not in terms of who can weigh the least but in terms of who is shapeliest, strongest, most agile, has the greatest stamina and the lowest percent body fat. Starvation diets are out; good, healthy nutrition is in.

I've noticed myself reflecting these changes. When I first started the *Bodysculpture* program my weight was an obsession. I weighed myself every morning, sometimes two or three times a day. A gain of ½ pound sent me into despair; a loss of 1 pound made my day. I was terrified of eating a normal meal, afraid that I'd go on a roll right back to 185 pounds if I gained so much as an ounce.

My fears were justified, at least statistically. Of the millions of Americans who lose 10 pounds or more each year, more than 90 percent of them regain the lost pounds, often with interest, in the 6 months following the end of the diet. I knew that I was on dangerous territory, and I reacted by being hyperconscious of my diet.

But slowly, I learned that I could relax a little. I passed the danger period of the critical first year, then the second, then the third. Five years after the initial big weight loss, I decided I could consider myself "cured." I found that weight watching was simply part of my daily routine, like showering or brushing my teeth. I did it almost as a matter of course, but it no longer occupied so much of my time or emotional energy. I worked out, watched my sugar, salt, and fat intake as well as my portion size—and found I could eat almost anything in small quantities. I also began to allow myself short holidays from dieting—special meals or celebrations, vacations or business trips, holiday meals when I went to visit my family. At worst, I'd put on a pound or two, which I would then lose after a couple of days back on my routine.

There is one other change that has taken place in our culture that is perhaps the most encouraging sign of all. We're finally coming out of the closet and admitting that women do (gasp) reach the age of 30 and still continue to function as attractive, sexual, energetic, active, strong people. Today's female sex symbol is not the bubble-headed nymphet; we also admire the woman who's fully grown-up and happy about it.

And that, too, is a big shift away from the pre-*Bodysculpture* era. When the book first appeared, interviewers shied away from the admission that the woman shown lifting the weights was (gasp) over 25. One magazine even rejected an excerpt on the grounds that its explicit editorial policy was to feature only women from 18 to 28. They had assumed from my pictures that I was about 26. When an unthinking publicist revealed that I was over 29, they killed the story.

I was mystified by the editorial policy. I looked half a decade younger than I actually was—and weight training had made it possible. What a discovery for women everywhere! But a magazine's editorial policy prevented its readers from learning the secret. I was terrifically proud of the fact that I looked and felt so much better in my thirties than I had in my overweight teens and twenties. But it was a sin for a woman to be over 30, no matter how good she looked! I developed a keen sense of irony in a hurry.

But now the pendulum has swung in the other direction again, and I hope that in some small way the *Bodysculpture Plus* program can help this movement along. Don't worry about your age, sisters. Just be the best possible version of you.

People often say to me after reading that first "Fight with the Fat Demon" story, "Losing all that weight really changed your life, didn't it?" I'm always somewhat taken aback at the question. But looking back over the five years that have passed, I have to admit they're right. It wasn't a single precipitous change but many small changes that have added up to a real difference in my life. As I lost the weight I became more confident of myself, more animated, less withdrawn. I began striking out, exploring, trying new things that, as a former fat girl, I had never had the courage to try. And I have no reservations whatsoever about saying that I would not be where I am today if I had not hauled out the barbells that winter day nearly seven years ago.

I've done a variety of things in that time period. I'm no longer a full-time academic person, although I still teach university courses part time for the fun of it. Ralph and I now have our own writing company, Words Unlimited, a technical and business communications firm. The early sale of *Bodysculpture* enabled us to realize a lifelong dream and become full-time writers. In addition to *Bodysculpture,* we've done 5 books in 5 years—2 for St. Martin's Press (*Bodypower* and *Sportspower*), and nearly 30 other book-length manuscripts for clients.

Some of our projects have been health- and beauty-oriented—such as the project we did for our friend Junius Risner, an innovative Chicago fashion designer, in which I was the photo model. We've also done textbooks and training manuals for model agencies and cosmetic companies, fashion and beauty columns for magazines, and we are currently starting an "In and Out in Chicago" column for *Crain's Chicago Business.*

I've also trained with an intensity that I would never have thought possible a decade ago. I now do repetition half squats with 305 pounds and bench press over 100 pounds at a body weight of 110. Ralph and I train together (same program) on Mondays, Wednesdays, and Fridays; on alternate days I get up for an early-morning run of 4 to 7 miles. We've done numerous seminars and workshops on fitness and weight loss for women, and I've had an opportunity I only dreamed of five years ago: a chance to talk with other women about their private frustrations, goals, dreams, and fears in their battles with the Fat Demon. We even had that 26-week television miniseries in Houston with Marijane Vandiver on KTRK. And, of course, we've traveled and promoted our other books in major cities all across the country.

As if this weren't enough, I'm involved in other activities, too. I keep up my scholarly reading and research, write articles and poetry, am an officer in my professional association, maintain an active involvement with women's groups and networks in Chicago, and work with adult education programs at the Church of the Ascension. But I fight my workaholism from time to time by watching Woody Allen movies, having tea with my friends, people-watching from Melvin's porch (while wearing my size 6 jeans), listening to old Beatles records, and managing an occasional quiet evening with the love of my life, who happens to be my coauthor and workout and business partner.

As you may have guessed, I look quite different nowadays. Unlike the first *Bodysculpture,* in which we weren't allowed to include the "before" and "after" photos (the editor didn't think anybody would believe them), this time we're putting them in so you can see how I've literally changed my shape. As I've continued training, I've not only lost body fat but have continued to reshape my body. Thanks to a heavy upper-body routine, which I began only four years ago, my bust has actually increased by an inch!

My shoulders and back have improved in definition, my waist is smaller, my tummy flatter (you can actually see some abdominal definition now), and my hips have dropped from their all-time high of 47 inches to 33½. My thighs are 17 inches and my calves, once over 16 inches, are now a reasonable 11½. Boots, once a no-no because of my chronically swollen legs, are a staple of my wardrobe. And clothes these days come in sizes 4, 5, and 6, with an occasional 7–8 in junior sizes. Designer jeans all seem to fit—the problem is deciding which ones to buy!

But I think that the biggest change has been my attitude toward the workouts themselves. No longer are the exercise sessions just a means to an end; they're ends in themselves. I've come to value my workouts in the gym as times when I can get in sync with my body and its new shape. They're times when I can push, test, experiment. Can I do one more rep? Two more? Another whole set? Add weight to this exercise? Do this one a new way? Switch from machines to free weights, or vice-versa? I like the feel of the barbell in my hands, like to push against the metal bar and feel it go up, sometimes against my own expectations. I like the feeling of having set a new record in a lift or of having improved my form. I enjoy the sense that I'm strong, faster on my feet, more graceful than ever before in my life.

And I also like the sense that for the first time in my life, I'm not afraid of mirrors. When I go into dressing rooms now, I stand for long minutes watching that reflection—but now I'm looking for firm leanness or critically examining the definition in my upper back or thighs. I'm constantly striving to look even better, but at the same time I'm fundamentally happy with what I see. In short, for the first time in my life, I like me—and that frees up an enormous amount of energy for friends, family, work, writing, and answering fan mail about *Bodysculpture*.

For, best of all, through all the changes, the original *Bodysculpture* has continued to sell. And that's a story in itself.

When we sat down on my parents' sun porch and started the chapter that eventually turned into the original "Fight with the Fat Demon," we had no idea what we were starting. To us the idea seemed perfectly simple and straightforward: if you want to reshape your body, use resistance training. But as we began to talk with editors, we realized that the idea was revolutionary. The book sold out the first printing in less than a month. There was something there that women wanted, and they proved it by buying the book and using its program to work out.

Just as we were packing and training for our West Coast tour, we got word that the tour was canceled because—we later learned—our publisher had engaged a celebrity male bodybuilder to write (or have written) a competitive book to be brought out later that year. Same publisher, same publicist! And although it was still selling, the publicity on the book was halted and no more printings were issued.

Thanks to our agent, a farsighted editor with another publisher, and an audience of women who knew what they wanted, the book was revived in paperback nearly two years later. And once again, the sales figures climbed right up the charts. The original *Bodysculpture* has now sold nearly 100,000 copies and is still selling.

Meanwhile, male and female bodybuilders, major and minor celebrities, TV stars and starlets, and aspiring soap opera heroines all hopped on the bandwagon we started way back in 1979. The market was flooded with exercise books for women—some good, some not so good, and some bad jokes. It was both frustrating and rewarding to watch it all happen—rewarding because it so raised people's consciousness about the legitimacy of exercise and fitness for women; frustrating because the same women's magazines that two years earlier had turned down excerpts from *Bodysculpture* because of the "freakiness" of weight training for women and young-slanted editorial policies now all featured over-40 movie and TV soap opera stars working out with weights.

But through it all, through all the plethora of celebrity books and hype and ballyhoo, *Bodysculpture* continued to sell. Booksellers, publicists, and editors alike were amazed. But I think I know the reason. Readers like yourselves understood that it was a real book about a real woman; not a packaged celebrity but a real woman like yourselves who got up in the morning and worked out with barbells while the coffee was brewing, who went to work with Baggies full of raw vegetables and came home in the evening and trained again while dinner cooked, and sometimes carried wet leotards to work in her briefcase straight from the gym. No hype, no star-studded cast, no media event—just a woman like themselves who had discovered a way to fight the Fat Demon and win.

I think that's the secret to the book's success. And I know that's the reason we're sitting down to write this one. In the past five years we've learned a tremendous amount that will help you in your own fight with the Fat Demon (yes, he's still around!). We've learned facts about nutrition, diet, exercise routines, equipment, specific exercises, and using fashion to dress lean and look lean while the new figure is in the making.

It's all here, and we want to share it with you, our readers.

So I'll end this chapter the way I ended the first story in *Bodysculpture:*

I fought the Fat Demon.

And I won. I'm still winning.

And so can you.

All it takes is your weights, a good diet, this book, and a lot of determination. You'll make it. I did. You will, too.

So keep reading. This is only the beginning.

Valerie "after" at 110 lbs.

Chapter 3

Getting Body and Soul
Together for
Maximum Progress

Body Politics

Most people seem to start their workouts in either of two ways: they drag the equipment out at home, give a deep sigh, and start exercising; or they drag themselves down to a health club, take a deep breath, and start exercising. In either case, they rarely warm up before launching into the workout much less prepare themselves mentally for the exercises they do.

We've seen a parade of injuries at gyms caused by the desire to get in, get to work, get through, and get out. Stiff or unused muscles are pulled, ligaments and tendons are stretched, and soreness follows the next day. For many, the pain the day after is proof enough that all this working out is madness—a sure sign that they should forget the whole thing.

Two things are wrong with this approach to exercise. First, *nobody* should work out without a warm-up, especially if you're doing heavy resistance or strenuous aerobic training. Exercise is a shock to the system, particularly if you're out of shape. If you are starting an exercise program because you're overweight, the odds are that you *are* out of shape. A warm-up prepares your body for what's coming. It's like getting into a cold pool—you don't just jump in all at once without some preparation.

Second, you need a mental "warm-up," too. When we wrote the original *Bodysculpture*, we included a little section we called "Psyching Up." It proved to be one of the most popular parts of the book. In a nutshell, we advised people to make exercise something special—not just a chore or something to which they were condemned because they wanted to lose weight but something good, fine, and fun.

Exercise programs alone won't sustain your interest indefinitely. Most people begin to lose interest when they see their target weight approaching. Often the problem here is that they look upon the workout as a necessary evil and not as a glorious communion between their minds and bodies. You can't have a successful exercise program unless you're mentally prepared for it. And you'll never sustain the effort required to reach your goals until you come to understand that exercise isn't drudgery but an opportunity to pull your body and soul together into a new you.

In *Bodysculpture* we described how to psych up for a workout. In *Bodysculpture Plus* we want to take the next step. We want to not only guide you into a good workout but show you how to sustain the program as well. You may know that over 90 percent of the women who lose weight through diets gain it all back within six months to a year after they lose it. We don't want this to happen to you.

Let's look at the physical aspects of staying on the program first. Then we'll turn to the psychological aspects. Here is a list of tips you can put into action:

1. *Always remember that exercise is a privilege, not a chore.* Ask anybody who has a heart condition or is confined to a wheelchair if he or she wouldn't prefer to be out jogging, swimming, playing tennis, working out, or otherwise leading an active life. The opportunity to jump, run, swim, push this marvelous body of ours and feel it respond is a God-given privilege for which we should all be thankful. We should never look upon it as a chore to be avoided.

2. *If you're chronically tired or have a physical disability, see your doctor!* If you are an otherwise normal person but feel chronically listless, you may have any of a number of ailments, some easy to correct and some serious. You may have low blood sugar or you may be suffering the after-effects of childhood rheumatic fever. You may be dieting or working out too strenuously. If you have no energy at the end of the day, you probably need more food and less exercise. If you're tired when you wake up, you may have other problems that need a physician's attention.

3. *Don't overdiet!* Overdieting takes many forms. The extremes are *anorexia nervosa* (self-imposed but involuntary starvation) and *bulimia* (alternately gorging oneself with food, then vomiting it up). If you have either of these problems, see your doctor and be honest with him or her about what you're doing.

   Don't starve yourself just to be able to get into a certain dress by a certain date. When you do this, the goal ceases to be losing weight and looking good and becomes merely being able to get into the dress. It's a false-trail. Don't get on it.

4. *Don't fad-diet!* Don't fall for all the fad diets that promise you the moon. They all operate on one principle: the total ignorance of the dieter concerning nutritional needs and the way the body works. By now everybody should know how these diets really work. You're 40 pounds overweight and you want to lose 10 pounds in two days? Simple. Cut out all carbohydrates.

   Carbohydrates bind two to three times their mass in water. For every ounce of carbohydrate you take in, you hang on to two or three ounces of water. Discontinue the carbohydrates and your body will let go of the water. Are you losing weight? Yes. Are you losing body fat? No. Will you gain the weight back? Yes. Just drink several glasses of water and eat some carbohydrates and the water weight will be right back. Progress? Zilch! Don't fall for it.

5. *Don't mono-diet!* Occasionally somebody will resurrect the old idea of eating only *one* kind of food. Take your pick: only papaya, only pineapple, only beef, only chicken, only vegetables, only green vegetables, only nuts, only honey—only, only, only. Will you lose weight? You bet. Why? You're suffering from malnutrition.

6. *Don't fast-diet!* Every year a few more people read the nutritional fringe literature and try fasting to lose weight. What happens when you fast? Your body starts feeding on itself. And not just on the fat but on the protein, too—so you're getting weaker and weaker.

   Your heart and nervous system also get weaker since you've cut out both protein and carbohydrates. If you have a heart condition or a neurological problem, fasting could kill you. Will you be thin? you bet! Will you look good? Do starving children look good?

7. *Beware of the one-note exercise program.* Although the original *Bodysculpture* program was primarily made up of resistance exercises, we included a marvelous set of Japan Karate Association stretching exercises for flexibility workouts and warm-ups before resistance sessions. In any exercise program you need routines for strength as well as endurance, speed, and agility as well as power.

8. *Remember that specificity is one of the fundamental principles of exercise physiology.* What this means is that if you want to gain in power and strength, you have to lift heavy weights. If you want to gain in endurance and develop cardiovascular conditioning, you have to work out aerobically: reach a target pulse rate and keep it there for 15 minutes or more.

You will *not* build strength in your arms by running or jogging, no matter what the people who promote jogging say. You will *not* get any cardiovascular conditioning by doing 3 or 4 repetitions of the exercise movements with heavy weights, no matter how muscular you may look. And don't think you're going to build endurance or strength by doing Yoga in slow motion.

9. *Don't be overly impressed by criticisms of one kind of exercise by the promoters of another kind of exercise.* Several years ago we heard a nationally known jogging enthusiast describe how he had made a monkey out of a champion bodybuilder by wearing him out in only 7 minutes on a treadmill. He used this story to invalidate weight training as an exercise method and to promote his own choice of exercise: running. It was a smoke screen. He never mentioned the specificity of exercise, which, of course, would have weakened his case.

The facts are simple, as you can deduce from 8 above. Unless the bodybuilder had trained specifically for endurance, there was no reason to expect him to be able to sustain a long cardiovascular workout. In the interest of fairness, the good doctor should have mentioned that he himself couldn't have lasted 7 seconds (much less 7 minutes!) with the amount of weight the bodybuilder lifted over and over again in his regular workouts.

10. *Know what you want and train for it.* This, of course, is a corollary of 8 and 9 above. The principle is simplicity itself. There is absolutely no mystery, regardless of what the hucksters would like you to think. Here's how it works:

   (a) *Want to build endurance and get cardiovascular conditioning at the expense of power and strength?* Eat a reasonable, balanced diet with enough carbohydrates to keep you going, and go on a daily running or jogging routine in which you reach your target pulse rate and sustain it for more than 15 minutes.

   (b) *Want to build brute strength at the expense of speed and endurance?* Do a slow, leisurely total-body workout with heavy weights and low repetitions every other day or three

to four times a week, pack in the proteins and carbohydrates, and forget about running or jogging.

(c) *Want to develop power (speed coupled with explosive
strength)?* Work out with heavy weights, low repetitions,
going as fast as you can in the contraction portion of each
exercise movement. Forget about running or jogging. Eat
extra protein.

(d) *Want to lose weight without losing strength or endurance?*
Cut down on your calorie intake, eat a balanced diet, do a
total-body resistance workout every other day, supplement
your resistance workout with aerobic activities (dancing,
jogging, running, skating, cross-country skiing, etc.)

(e) *Want to shape your body; lose fat; build strength, power,
speed, and endurance; increase flexibility and gracefulness;
look and feel younger than you have in years without
sacrificing one ounce of your femininity?* Follow the Bodysculpture Plus *program.* It's a balanced, easy-to-follow syn-
thesis of all the ingredients you need.

11. *Don't fall for the vitamin, protein, and mineral supplement scam.*
Protein and mineral supplements for athletes are a multibillion-
dollar business. Do you need them? Probably not, unless you're
overdieting. If you are dieting strenuously enough to need mineral
supplements to make up for what you're not getting in your food,
your local pharmacy can give you all you need for a few dollars. Also
keep in mind that iron is iron and vitamin C is vitamin C regardless
of the special claims made by manufacturers in female-oriented
advertising.

12. *Don't try to do ultraflexibility movements just because the movie
stars do them.* Flexibility is a matter of how your joints are made.
Joints consist of a systematic structuring of ligaments (which hold
the bones together), tendons (which fasten the muscles to the bones
and snake around the joints), cartilage (which provides support and
movement surfaces), and fluid (between the moving parts).

Some people are hyperflexible and others aren't. Sometimes it's
not a matter of getting into shape but of how your joints are made.
Don't injure yourself just because some limber-jointed celebrity
makes a show of lifting her foot as high as her shoulders. Such
contortions neither burn fat nor shape the body. They can, however,
undermine the structural integrity of your joints.

13. *If you join a health club, don't let them push you around.* You pay
the same fees as the men, therefore have the same rights as the

men. If you want the things listed in *10 (e)* above, you'll need weights as well as the running track or stationary bikes. If they tell you that women shouldn't work out with weights, ask for your money back. If they won't give it back, either sue them or take the case to the state attorney's office. Sex discrimination is against the law. Don't let them get away with it.

Soul Searching

In addition to getting your physical act together, if you want to succeed with your *Bodysculpture Plus* program, you've also got to learn how to handle your psyche. Here are a few tips that will help you develop the mental discipline you need:

1. *Build a new self-image.* You've simply got to create an affirmative self-image. There's a mind-set as well as a body type that goes with being fat or lean. Part of the point of developing a regimen like the one in this book is to change your head as well as your body. In other words, you must change the self-image you've developed as a fat person.

   What is the new mind-set? It's positive instead of negative, for one thing. The fat mind-set says, "I hate my body. I'm at war with it. It's not me. I'm uncomfortable moving and living in it, so I move as little as possible—and when I do, I'm ill at ease."

   The lean mind-set says, "I like me. I like my body, and I'm comfortable with it. My body is not separate from but is part of me, and I accept it, with all its flaws and imperfections. I'm happy being me. I love to move with my body. I love to do my exercises, to walk, to run, to move, and to dance."

   That's the difference we mean. And you can help yourself develop it. But it takes time. We're learning more about the importance of self-image every day. Physicians and psychiatrists have known for many decades that formerly fat people often continue to think of themselves as fat even when they are positively emaciated. In other words, the body image often doesn't change along with your actual body size and shape.

   Result: you feel fat, even when you're normal size or even underweight. This is the problem with many anorexics and bulimics; their body weight has dropped to a point far below normal, yet they still "feel" and "see" themselves as overweight. So they diet and diet and diet, often with lethal effects.

2. *Get rid of your obsession with thinness.* The obsession with thinness has become a sort of national neurosis for women. In a poll reported in the February 1984 issue of *Glamour* magazine, 75 percent of the female respondents felt that they were too fat, although only 25 percent were actually overweight. And twice as many women answered that "losing ten pounds" would make them happier than succeeding in a career or meeting the "right" man.

Overweight is bad, particularly when its 20 pounds or more over your "normal" or "ideal" weight. In our "thin is in" culture it's all too easy to go to the other extreme. While it may be true that you can't be too rich, you certainly *can* be too thin, as millions of anorexia nervosa victims can testify.

It's also all too easy to let weight become the focal point of your life. As a result, your life comes to be dominated by the scale and the numbers it registers. And in dealing with that all-consuming obsession you can neglect other, more important aspects of your life: career, family, friends, involvement in larger issues, even the needs of your own spirit and psyche.

So don't do it! In the process of losing weight, try to maintain some sense of balance and harmony in your life. The Greeks had a word for this balance: *paideia,* the harmony of body and soul, expressed in the phrase "a sound body and a sound mind." That's the goal you're striving for, not a particular number on the bathroom scale or even the fit of a pair of size 6 designer jeans.

3. *Learn to communicate with your body.* What are you doing right now besides reading this line? Is your right foot still or is it twitching? Do your ears itch? Are your eyes tired? Has your leg gone to sleep? What signals is your body sending you right now? Fatigue? Aches? Are you really alive or are you ignoring all the messages your body sends your mind? Learn to listen to your body.

4. *Learn to communicate with your emotions.* Just as we easily get out of touch with the signals the body gives us, we also lose touch with what our emotions tell us. What do you bring with you to the experiences you have? Do you start your exercise program with the attitude that it probably won't work or do you start each workout with the feeling that this is going to be the best one yet? Take stock of how you really feel about the things you see and hear and do every day. Are you unhappy about them? Are you resigned or indif-

ferent? Are you "down" all the time? Do you have trouble keeping your initiative up? If your answer to these questions is yes, no wonder you have trouble staying on a program!

5. *Learn to communicate with your mind.* Sounds silly, doesn't it? It's easy to see how we might lose touch with our bodies and emotions, but our mind is always with us. Well, it's not that simple. Think of your mind as the executive of the compound organism that you call "you." Your mind is the center of your consciousness, and it's the boss that calls the shots. Or is it?

Consider this: do you do what you know is best for you or are you always a victim of emotional binges or physical laziness? When you see a 4,000-calorie dessert, do you do what your rational mind tells you to do or do you give way to that part of you that is perfectly willing to throw away all your progress for one taste of chocolate (or buttered popcorn, or a candy bar, or lasagna, or pizza), or any of the thousands of other temptations that come our way every time we really begin to make some progress?

6. *Learn to communicate with the world around you.* Don't become a hermit just because you don't look the way you think you ought to look. You're on the way to making some big changes in your life. Look beyond yourself to the world around you. Think about how the new you is going to enjoy a new life in that world.

7. *Gain control over yourself.* We've said that you have to get in touch with your emotions and your mind as well as your body. The purpose of these two suggestions is to teach you to gain control over yourself. But we are not suggesting that you become psychologically self-indulgent. Just the opposite! By learning to control yourself— your emotions and your mind—you'll be able to take the next step, which is to get yourself out of the way so you can make some progress.

How do you do that? The answer comes from a surprising source. One day last year we were listening to a sermon by Michael Marshall, then the bishop of Woolwich, England. Bishop Marshall was visiting our church as part of a tour of American churches, and everybody turned out to hear what he had to say. The bishop is an internationally acclaimed dynamic speaker, and we were all on the edge of our seats.

The single most arresting bit of advice we were given was also the simplest. Bishop Marshall was describing what one had to do in order to change one's life for the better. His advice was, "GET LOST!"

What he meant was this: most of us undercut our own progress, no matter what we're trying to do, because we spend all of our creative energies looking at ourselves. We can't see the path in front of us because we ourselves are in the way. We become so preoccupied with ourselves that we can't see the solutions to our problems. So what is it that gets in the way of our personal progress most of the time? Us. Ourselves. We do, that's who.

8. *Put everything else out of your mind and think about the real reasons you haven't succeeded.* What do you see? You see youself. We always seem to stand in the way of our own progress:

- We can't lose weight because we're always worrying about how we look.
- We can't work out for worrying about how we look while we're working out.
- We can't get started on a program because we're worried about not being able to do the program.
- We can't control our desire to pig out because we can't get our desire to pig out off our minds.
- We can't concentrate on the exercises because we keep thinking about *ourselves* doing the exercises.
- We can't keep track of the program because we're always thinking about ourselves instead of the program.
- We can't control our emotions because we worry constantly about not being able to control our emotions.
- We can't discipline our minds because we ourselves are all that's on our minds.
- We can't get anywhere because we keep stumbling over ourselves.

9. *Escape yourself.* People always ask us how they can develop the self-discipline to sustain a workout program. We tell them to forget about themselves and concentrate on the program. Stop looking for instant results and experience the joy that comes from the program itself. Stop worrying about getting into a particular dress size and think about doing the most perfect bench press, the most perfect leg extension, the most perfect run you've ever done. In short, GET LOST!

But isn't it yourself that all of this is being done for? Of course it is. We're talking about strategies for success. For example, which is the better way to learn to play a musical instrument—worrying constantly about whether or not you're going to be able to learn to play it or concentrating on the instrument itself?

The same goes for a host of other activities: riding a bicycle, driving a car, painting a landscape, or performing a ballet. If you spend all of your time worrying about YOU, you'll never learn how to do the thing you're trying to do.

Therefore, a fundamental rule is: If you want to succeed in your exercise program, you've got to get yourself off your mind so you can concentrate on what you're doing. We're completely serious about all of this for the same reason that Bishop Marshall was serious about it. After all he, too, was talking about getting body and soul together.

10. *Never think of exercise as something completely apart from the rest of your life.* It should be something special, but it shouldn't be divorced from the rest of your activities. Staying in trim, lean, beautiful condition is a way of life, not something you do in your spare time.

11. *Make your workouts important for their own sake.* When we go to the health club three times a week we look forward to seeing the regulars who work out alongside us. For them as for us, workouts are something to look forward to, something to relish, something to give our day that extra bit of momentum that wouldn't be possible otherwise.

12. *Enjoy the social aspects of working out, but don't become dependent on a workout partner to make your program work.* Few things are more rewarding than having a good workout partner. We've worked out together almost daily for more than 10 years. But neither of us depends on the other to provide the psychic energy needed for the workout. We *do* provide it for each other, but it's never taken for granted. Otherwise, one person is working and the other is dragging. Make it *your* workout, and you'll make it work.

13. *Develop a ritual that will help you make the transition from just sitting around to working out.* You should make your workout program a part of your life, but you also need to make it special. The best way to do this is to have a ritual that helps you make the transition from your ordinary activities to the workout. That's what the next section of this chapter is about.

A Rite of Passage

Again, there's nothing mysterious about all this, it's just common sense. The first task in any workout, as Woody Allen said about being on television, is to show up. If you're going to go through a workout, you first have to show up. So either get dressed and get down to the gym or drag the equipment out of the spare room and let's get ready to get to work. Here are some tips on making the transition to the workout if you're exercising at home:

1. *Preliminary preparations*
   (a) Have a regular place in which to work out. It may be the garage, a spare room, the basement, the porch, or a bedroom. The important thing is to work out in the same location each time. It will give you a sense of place and allow you to concentrate on the workout instead of on the hassle of figuring out where you're going to work out today.
   (b) Have a regular workout suit, whether it's a leotard, a sweatsuit, or a loose-fitting pair of slacks. Be sure that you have complete freedom of movement.
   (c) Pull out the barbell set and any other equipment you will use in the workout. Go ahead and set it up for the first exercise. Have everything ready so you won't have to interrupt your train of thought when you start to exercise.
   (d) Tack, pin, or tape your workout routine to the wall so you can refer to it during the workout without having to rummage through a notebook.
   (e) Lay out your copy of *Bodysculpture Plus* for each reference in case you forget how to do one of the exercises.

2. *The transition*
   Okay, you're all ready to go. Before you do any exercise movements, do the following:
   (a) Lie down on the floor or the bed and let your arms lie straight, elbows slightly bent, at an angle from the body. Spread your legs slightly. Make sure that you are completely comfortable. Put a pillow under your head if you like.
   (b) Close your eyes. Don't think about your weight problem or any other problems. Relax . . . relax.
   (c) Concentrate on your breathing. Relax until your breathing is regular and easy. Then forget about your breathing and turn to your heartbeat.
   (d) Listen to your heartbeat and feel your way into its natural rhythms. Then forget about your heartbeat.

(e) Imagine that your body is disappearing. You can feel it go. First your hands and arms, then your feet and legs, then your torso, then your head. Let your body go. Leave your body. Get out of it. Forget about it.

(f) Now turn your attention away from yourself. Try to forget about that "you" that seems to be the source of so many problems. Try to form images in your mind of the most tranquil scene you can think of. But don't think about yourself experiencing that scene. Just experience it, step into it, feel your way into it, and forget about your "self" and concentrate on what you're going to do.

(g) It's now time to come back, but as a different person. Think and feel your way back into your body. First listen for your heartbeat, then for your breathing. Move your fingertips, then your toes, then your arms, then your legs, then your torso.

(h) Feel the strength in this body you are filling. Stretch its arms and legs, bend its torso.

(i) Now unify yourself with your body, open your eyes, and stand up. You're a new person. You aren't thinking about yourself at all. You're thinking about the workout, the exercises, and the joy of feeling your muscles work in unison with your heart and lungs. You feel full of strength and power. You can do anything! You're a unity of body and soul—not separate but one.

3. *The workout*

   (a) Start the warm-up exercises, then go right into the workout. Give it everything you've got. Do each exercise as if this is the last time you'll ever have the privilege of doing these wonderful movements with your body.

   (b) Concentrate on each exercise movement. Make each one the best you've ever done, each movement your personal best.

   (c) Let your inward light shine forth and fill everything you do. Treasure every moment of the workout.

4. *The road back*

   (a) When you've finished the workout, sit down on the floor in a comfortable position and close your eyes. When your breathing and heartbeat have returned to normal, lie back and let your arms and legs relax.

(b) Listen to your body. Listen to the ocean sound in your ears, to the fullness of your breathing, to the strength of your heartbeat.

(c) Feel your way through every inch of your body. Marvel at the way it is working, at what it has done. Appreciate the miracle of your body.

(d) Now leave your body just as you did the last time. Get out of it and go once more to that quiet place where you left your "self."

(e) It's again time to go back. Reintegrate yourself and your body. Feel its quiet strength again. Open your eyes, stand up, and look around you.

(f) Try to retain the same unification between body and soul you enjoyed during the workout. Work on it. Keep it. Forget about your "self" and think about maintaining the perfect unity between body and soul. Do this and your "self" will never get in your way again.

5. *Working out in a gym or health club*

(a) Although nothing would help them more than the rite of passage we've described above, most people at health clubs just walk in, warm up, and start their workout without any mental preparation at all. Don't let the fact that you're in a gym prevent you from making the transition you need to make.

(b) Find a section of floor space and do the transition ritual described on the previous page. If anybody wants to know what you're doing, show them this book and tell them to read this section. You'll probably find them doing the same thing the next time you come to the gym.

(c) Remember that health clubs are only incidentally built to provide you with a place to work out. Health clubs exist primarily for the purpose of selling health club memberships. If the club you belong to or are planning to join is one that insists on "organized" exercise classes, be aware that the chief reason for the organized classes is to get you out of the club in a hurry in order to make room for the next group. Don't let them do it to you. Proceed at your own pace. You are *not* cattle. Don't let them treat you as if you were.

6. *Après workout*

When you've finished your workout, take full advantage of the fact that you feel terrific. Now's the time to give your body loving care with creams and powder, shampoo and rinse, and terrific-looking clothes. When you come out of the health club locker room or your home bathroom, you should look like the new person you're becoming.

Look in the mirror. What do you see? Can you detect the change that is coming over you? As the weeks go by, the person in the mirror will look more and more like the person you *really* are—that person who is a perfect unity of body and soul. You are in control of yourself, now. Your "self" no longer stands in the way of the plans that *you* have for your future.

You're on your way now, and nothing can stop you!

Chapter 4

Exercises for
Flexibility and Agility

Warm-Up

Flexibility exercises can also be used for warm-ups and cool-downs. Nobody should launch into the workout without a good warm-up; likewise, nobody should stop exercising without a cool-down to bring herself back down to earth. If she does, she is likely to injure herself with anything from strained tendons to torn muscles. The whole idea of *Bodysculpture Plus* is to shape the body while promoting speed, agility, gracefulness, strength, and endurance. In addition to looking good, you're going to *be* good, too. So the last thing you need is the hassle of having to deal with injuries.

In the original *Bodysculpture* we advised women who were new to exercise to do a stretching and limbering routine as a warm-up and as their initiation into the program. The warm-up we described is the body-conditioning routine used by the All America Karate Federation to strengthen the joints, provide flexibility for the various karate techniques, and give overall light conditioning to the body.

In this chapter we're going to give you several choices for flexibility and agility training, each of which will also provide you with the warm-up or cool-down you need before and after doing either resistance work or aerobics.

First, let's go over the karate stretch routine. It's still the best all-around flexibility warm-up we know. We've worked out some new variations on the exercises that will make them even more effective. Don't

47

worry yet about how many times you're supposed to do the movements. We'll cover that in the chapter on programs. For now, let's just learn how to do them.

Karate Flexibility Exercises

HEAD ROLLS
As you will learn from your workouts, your neck is probably a lot stiffer than you thought it was. Many of the lifts, such as the shoulder shrug and squats with the bar behind the neck, will make the neck feel even stiffer. You can't be very graceful with a stiff neck, so let's loosen up a bit.

Front and Back Roll
Stand erect, hands resting on the hips, and bow your head as far as you can. Try to touch your chin to your chest. Now slowly move your head backward and try to touch your upper back with the back of your head. At first you may not be able to do the full movement, but this is what you should work toward.

Front head roll    **Back head roll**

Revolving Roll

A word of caution about this one: if you are out of shape or have problems with balance, you may get dizzy at first when you do this exercise. Further, some people complain of popping noises in their necks when they do the movement. The popping noises are usually harmless, but if the exercise hurts, don't do it! Try it slowly at first until you can move freely.

Stand erect and imagine that your head is a ball that is attached to your torso by a thick, pliable cable. Bend your head forward until your chin is against your chest. Roll your head to the right, keeping the chin down. As you round your right shoulder, lift your chin so that the back of the head rolls along the top of the upper back. As you round the left shoulder, bring the chin back down and continue to roll your head until your chin is down against the top center of your chest again. Now do the same movement in the opposite direction.

UPPER BACK AND PECTORAL STRETCHES

Now it's time to move down from the neck to the upper back. Stand erect for these exercises.

Straight-Arm Overhead Stretch

Extend your arms overhead and clasp your hands together. Keep your elbows straight but not quite locked. Now arch your back and lean backward as far as you can while pulling your arms back in the direction of the movement. You'll feel your latissimus muscles (muscles in the middle back which curve around to the sides under the arms) stretch on this one, and you will also feel the muscles at the base of your neck bunch up.

Straight-Arm Stretch to the Sides

Extend your arms in front of you, palms facing each other, then bring them back, elbows almost locked, until the arms are at the sides as far as they will go. The arc made by the arms should be parallel to the floor. In this exercise you will work both the chest and the upper back muscles.

Bent-Arm Shrug

Stand erect, with your arms down by the sides, palms facing the rear. Raise your arms out to the sides, but bend the elbows as you raise them.

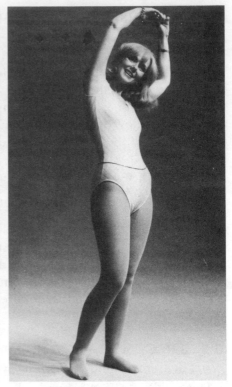

Straight-arm overhead stretch   **Straight-arm stretch to the sides**

When you've raised your arms as far as they will go, your forearms should be pointing down toward the floor. Raise the elbows as high as you can get them. This exercise will work the trapezius muscles of the upper back (which form the area between the neck and shoulders on either side of the head), as well as the lateral and posterior deltoids (side and back shoulder muscles). It will also stretch the latissimus muscles.

SHOULDER LOOSENERS

Now let's move from the neck and back down to the shoulders as we limber up from head to toes.

Windmills to the Sides

Stand erect, with your arms down by your sides. Start a propeller movement with the arms, keeping them in a plane perpendicular to the floor. Start swinging the arms to the front, then overhead, then to the rear, making a full circle. Start slowly and increase the speed as you count the repetitions. Now do the same movement in the opposite direction.

50

Bent-arm shrug   Windmills to the sides

Windmills to the Front

Now swing smoothly into a movement where the arms cross in front instead of making circles at the sides. Interweave the hands and forearms as your arms swing around to the front. Think of an eggbeater. Then do the same movement in the opposite direction.

WAIST WRINGERS

Your neck, upper back, chest, and shoulders are now warmed up. Let's move down to the waist. Remember that the waist is not just the tummy but includes the back and the sides as well.

Front Slumps

Bend slowly toward the front at the waist, as if you were going to tuck your head between your legs (which you may someday be able to do if you're naturally very flexible, but don't try it the first day). Don't bounce, and do the movement very slowly. This is a good stretch for the lower back, so if you have lower back problems you should be extra careful when you do this one.

51

 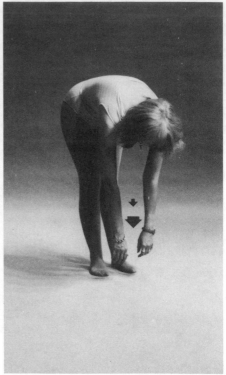

Windmills to the front   **Front slumps**

The point here is not to see how far down you can go. It's just to warm up the lower back muscles by providing them with a little natural stretch. When you've bowed forward as far as you can comfortably go, slowly raise back up until you are fully erect. With a smooth, unbroken movement, put your hands on your hips, arch your back, and lean backward as far as you can go. Hold for a count of three, then move toward the front again.

Seated Twists

Every day we see people wasting their time by doing twists while standing up. When you do this exercise standing up, the torso twists along its logitudinal axis and the waist gets practically no workout at all. The best way to do twists is in a seated position. That way, the hips are immobilized, and the work of twisting is concentrated in the side muscles (the external and internal obliques). Use a broomstick or a light bar for this one. Lay it across the shoulders behind the head and drape your arms over the bar. Don't saw the neck with the bar.

Seated twists

The Basic Crunch

This has become a popular exercise because it concentrates the effort on the abdominal muscles without the danger of lower back strain that is always present with regular sit-ups. In fact, you won't find sit-ups in this book. Avoid them and do the crunch instead.

To do the basic crunch, lie on the floor on your back and prop your feet up on a chair. Bend the knees about 90 degrees. Cross your arms in front of you on your chest. Raise your shoulders up off the floor as far as you can go while keeping the small of the back against the floor. Then hold the shoulders off the floor while raising the hips off the floor. This is a fairly complicated movement, but you'll get it in a few seconds. The whole idea is to shorten the distance between your breastbone (where the abdominal muscles are anchored at the top) and the pubic bone (where the abdominals are anchored at the bottom).

ARM STRETCHES AND FLEXES

Let's do the arms before we move on to the hips. Here are a few movements that will warm up the arms and wrists.

The basic crunch

Arm curl

Arm extension

Stand erect, with the arms down at the sides. Bend the arms at the elbows and slowly flex them until the fists are at shoulder height. As you bring the fists up, rotate the forearms so that your palms are facing your chest when the arm is fully bent. Then keep the elbows bent and raise the arms until they are alongside your head, with the elbows pointing toward the ceiling. Rotate the forearms again as you straighten your arms overhead. Hold for a count of three, then bring your arms back down the same way they went up until the elbows are straight and the arms are down at the sides.

Without interrupting the movement, keep moving the arms (with the elbows straight) behind you until they have gone as far as your shoulder joints will allow them to go. Hold for a count of three while bending the wrists back and forth. Then start the cycle over again. Concentrate on keeping the muscles in the front of the arms (the biceps) *and* the back of the arms (the triceps) contracted at the same time during each movement. Keep the tension going between these opposing muscle groups at all times during this exercise.

HIP HANGERS

By now you're warmed up all the way down to the hips. The hip muscles are essential both to running and to squatting exercises, so warming them up is as important as warming up any part of the body.

Front Leg Raises

Stand erect and extend your right arm in front of you, palm facing the floor. Bring your right leg up with the knee almost straight until the toe hits the palm of your right hand. Now repeat the movement with the left arm and leg. Put some force behind the swing. Really kick the palm of your hand! Concentrate on balance, speed, and agility.

The X-Rated Hip Exercise

This one was in the original *Bodysculpture* book and has proved to be a perennial favorite. It has advantages over the standing backswing of the leg, since the work is concentrated in the hip muscles (the *gluteus maximus*). Lie on the floor on your back with your feet pulled up as far toward the hips as they will go. Thrust the pelvis toward the ceiling as high as you can. Hold for a count of three before going back down to the floor.

Front leg raises

A variation on this one: lie with your upper back on a low bench and your hips hanging off the edge of the bench. Your back should be arched and your knees bent, feet flat on the floor, with your buttocks almost touching the floor. Thrust your pelvis toward the ceiling as far as it will

The X-rated hip exercises

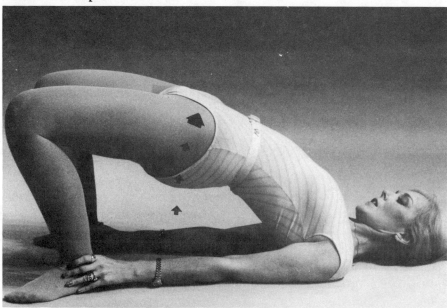

go. Then slowly return to the starting position. Be careful with this one because it will really work your lower back and abdomen as well as your hips.

Lateral Leg Raises

This one works the sides of the hips and the sides of the legs at the hip (the *gluteus medius* and *tensor fascia latae*). You can do this one either lying on the floor or standing. Let's describe the lying position first.

Lie on the floor on your right side. Keep the hips thrust forward and the back slightly arched. Raise your right leg directly toward the ceiling as high as it will go. *Don't allow yourself to roll to the back*. If you do, the work will be done by the front hip muscles instead of the side hip muscles. Repeat the movement with the other leg to work out the left side.

Lateral leg raises (lying)

Now let's do the standing version. With your right hand, grasp the back of a chair or a doorjamb to steady yourself. Raise your right leg to the side as high as it will go. You will find this version of the lateral leg raise more difficult than the lying version because the tension remains on the muscles at the highest point of the movement. Again, resist the urge to turn so that the front hip muscles are doing the lifting. Repeat the movement with the other leg.

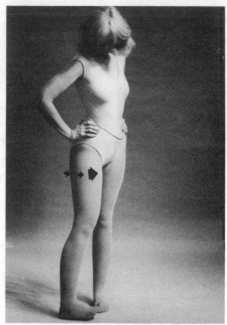

Lateral leg raises (standing)   Hip-joint twists

Hip-Joint Twists

Stand erect and lift the ball and toes of your right foot slightly off the floor, keeping the heel on the floor. The knee should be kept straight and locked. Look down at your right foot and slowly rotate your leg at the hip joint so that the toes point toward your left leg. Go as far as you can, hold for a count of three, then move in the opposite direction as far as you can go. Repeat the movement with the other leg. This will give a gentle workout to the hip rotators.

The Semi-Lotus Hip Stretch

Sit on the floor with your legs out in front of you, knees bent. Push your knees down in an arc to the sides and bring them as close to the floor as you can. At the end of the movement, the soles of your feet should be touching. Keep your back straight or slightly arched during the movement. Don't force your knees down, but do the movement gently. This will work the hip rotators. Be careful. Don't bounce!

HIP AND KNEE STRETCHES

These exercises work the hips and the knees. Don't bounce, and don't force your limbs past their natural range of motion.

The semi-lotus hip stretch

The Knee-Beater

This is a rough one if you're stiff or out of shape. Sit on the floor with your legs extended in front of you. The knees should *not* be bent. Your feet should be perpendicular to the floor, with the toes pointing to the

The knee beater

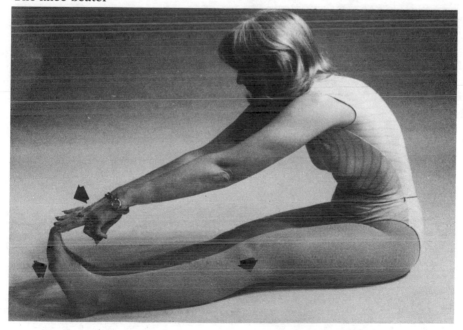

ceiling. Now lean forward and touch your toes without bending your knees. Can't do it? Don't worry. The idea here is to increase flexibility not to injure the lower back or the ligaments of the knee. Do the movement *gently* and *slowly*. Don't lunge forward.

The Ambivalent Frog

This is the toughest one of all. We call it the "ambivalent frog" because when you do it you'll look like a frog that can't decide which way to jump. It's a great hip and thigh exerciser. Squat down on the floor until your right leg is straight out to the side along the floor and the left leg is bent at the knee with the left foot under your hips. Reach over and place your right hand on your right knee. Don't push down but use your hand to steady yourself. If your ankles are stiff you'll have to rest on the ball of your left foot. Ideally, the left foot should be flat against the floor.

Now, without raising up any farther than is necessary to do the movement, shift your body to the right so that it is your left leg that is extended out to the side along the floor and your right leg that is doubled beneath you. Got the movement? Now shift from one leg to the other without standing up or falling down!

The ambivalent frog

FOOT ROTATIONS

Sit on the floor with your legs extended in front of you. Keep the knees locked. Bend your feet back toward you, then away from you as far as they will go. Rotate your feet at the ankles, first in one direction, then in the other.

Foot rotations

Foot rotations

Yoga Movements for Flexibility and Relaxation

The karate conditioning exercises you've just learned will help you become more agile, as well as providing you with a good preworkout warm-up. Now let's talk about some less strenuous oriental exercises that will give you flexibility, gracefulness of movement, body control, and a little relaxation. They can be used either at the beginning of the workout as a gentle warm-up or at the end of the workout as a cool-down.

While Yoga exercises (regardless of what practitioners may tell you) will *not* build strength or endurance, they *will* help you to learn proper breathing techniques and make you more flexible, coordinated, and fluid in your movements. The positions also serve as instant de-tensers completely apart from workouts, so you can use them in the morning or at night after a hard day's work. When we get to the chapter on programs, we'll show you how to incorporate them into a variety of aerobic or resistance exercises.

A few general words about Yoga movements before we begin. First of all, remember that the object is not speed or lifting a heavy mass but grace, flexibility, and coordination. Do each movement slowly, rhythmically, striving each time for a little more suppleness. Do each movement only to the extent that you do not feel pressure or pain. One of the popular Yoga movements, the "plough," is omitted here because of the danger of injury.

Remember, you're not in competition here. You aren't trying to set any lifting or speed records. Take it slow and easy, and move in a relaxed, unhurried manner. And learn to breathe properly—that is, deeply and rhythmically.

Ready? Let's try some simple warm-ups first as a prelude to the more difficult postures.

MEDITATION POSTURE

There are three postures here: the *easy posture,* the *half lotus,* and the *full lotus.*

The *easy posture* is done sitting cross-legged on the floor, one ankle crossed in front of the other, hands resting on the knees. As you sit,

Easy meditation posture

Half-lotus meditation posture

Full-lotus meditation posture

maintain the posture and breathe deeply for five breathing cycles, inhaling and exhaling slowly and deeply.

The *half lotus* is more advanced. Cross the legs so that the right ankle rests on the left thigh. Palms should rest easily on the knees. Again, take five breaths.

The most advanced posture is the *full lotus*. The ankle of each foot is placed atop the opposite thigh so that the legs are literally intertwined. Palms can rest on the knees or on the floor. Save this one for a more advanced stage of your training schedule unless you are already very supple and limber.

THE SUN GREETING

This is not only a warm-up but a complete series of exercises. It's an excellent combination of Yoga positions and deep-breathing sequences.

Here's a step-by-step guide. We'll number the steps for the sake of clarity.

1. Stand straight with the legs and hands together, fingers touching in a "prayer" position. As you stand, exhale all of the air from your lungs.
2. Inhale deeply. Raise your arms high above your head and then arch backward as far as you can.
3. As you exhale, bend forward slowly, reaching down as far as possible. Keep the feet together and don't bend the knees. But don't strain your back by reaching back too far. The object is not to touch the floor but to simply bend forward as far as you can do so comfort-

Sun greeting

ably. Be sure that you completely empty your lungs as you exhale.
4. Place your hands on the floor and assume a partially kneeling position (see photo). Inhale and bend your left leg up toward your chest as you step back onto the right leg. Keep your head up and remember to inhale deeply, completely filling your lungs with air.
5. Exhale as you step back into a push-up position. Stretch both legs out together so that your body is supported only by your hands and toes. Keep your body stiff and remember to exhale completely as you do so.
6. Continue exhaling as you lower first your knees, then your chest

Sun greeting

Sun greeting/cobra

and chin, to the floor. Try to keep it all one continuous motion. Arms
should be extended on the floor in front of you.

7. Now slide onto your stomach with your legs extended fully behind
you. Your chest and forehead should rest on the floor.
8. As you inhale, rise slowly into the *cobra position* by straightening
your arms. Keep your head and back up. Toes should be pointed,

feet together, thighs flat on the floor. Do the posture as fully as you can, but don't strain. Straighten your arms as far as you comfortably can and try for a little more each time.

9. Now begin exhaling as you lower yourself back to position (7) with your chin and chest on the floor.
10. Continue exhaling as you raise your hips up off the floor so that your body forms a triangle. Lock your chin into your chest, look at your feet, and try to force your heels all the way down to the floor.
11. Inhale again as you step forward with the right foot, backward on the left. This is the reverse of position 4, in which the left foot was forward and the right extended.
12. Exhale and bring the left leg forward beside the right leg. Bend and be sure to empty your lungs completely as you exhale.
13. Inhale again and return to position 2. Arms should be raised over the head and the back should be arched as far back as is comfortable.
14. As you inhale, repeat opening position 1. Relax for a few minutes now that the whole sun greeting has been completed.

CAT STRETCH

Start this position on your hands and knees. Exhale so that you completely empty your lungs of air. Squeeze the air out with your dia-

Cat stretch

phragm if necessary. As you inhale, pull your head back while lowering your chest and tummy toward the floor, keeping the feet together and the toes pointed.

Now exhale and bow your back like a cat. Bring the chin into the chest and keep the back bowed. As you inhale, extend your right leg back and upward. Arch your back and tilt your head back at the same time.

Exhale and bring the right leg forward. Bring the knee up into your chest, lower your head, and try to touch your nose with your knee. Repeat with the left leg.

After one repetition with each leg, relax into the *folded-leaf posture*: kneel on the floor, lower your chin to the floor, and extend your hands, palms up, behind you on either side. Hold this position for three complete breathing cycles and then rise slowly as you inhale.

SHOULDER STAND

This is a basic posture and a fine all-purpose energizer and relaxer. It aids circulation toward the heart and helps prevent fatigue and water retention in the lower legs.

Lie on your back with your arms at your sides. Exhale and then inhale, raising both legs slowly until they are perpendicular to the floor. Hold this position and exhale slowly as you hold it. Then inhale again,

Shoulder stand

raising your hips all the way off the floor. Support them with your hands for added balance.

This position is the *half-shoulder stand.* Hold the position for three complete breathing cycles, then try to straighten yourself to a completely vertical position (the *full-shoulder stand*). Hold this position for five more breathing cycles and then come down very slowly. It helps to roll your back slowly onto the floor so that you don't hurt yourself by bouncing.

THE COBRA

You should find this one easy since you have already incorporated part of this posture into your sun greeting exercise (Step 8). Lie on your stomach with your arms by your sides and relax. Exhale completely. Then, as you inhale, lift your head up off the floor and bring your palms to a position just under your shoulders. Support yourself on your arms. Now arch your back as far as possible to attain a good stretch. Don't go any farther than is comfortable—you should feel a stretch, but not a painful one. Hold the position for three complete breathing cycles. As you become more supple, try arching your back even more until you are supporting yourself on your palms only.

THE CAMEL

Begin by kneeling on the floor, sitting on your heels in an easy, erect posture. Rest your hands on your knees. Exhale completely, and as you inhale, rise up on your knees while swinging your arms behind your back. Stretch your arms as far back as they will go. Continue to inhale, and bring your arms up all the way behind your back and over your head. Stretch your whole body and gently start arching your back.

Exhale and lower your arms down by your sides so that they rest on your heels. Arch your back even farther and let your neck relax. Hold the position for three complete breathing cycles. Then relax into the folded-leaf posture for three more breaths to complete the exercise.

THE HARE

This posture is a counterstretch to back-bending postures like the cobra. Kneel on the floor, sitting on your heels, legs under you. Turn your toes down into the floor. First exhale, then inhale. As you exhale again, bend forward and pull your head toward your knees. Make sure

The camel

The hare

your back is as rounded as you can make it. Hold this position while you exhale all the air in your lungs. Hold for five seconds, then rise slowly as you inhale. Repeat three times, and on the third repetition, hold the head-into-knees posture for three complete breathing cycles.

THE FISH

This is a traditional counterstretch to the shoulder stand and should be done immediately after you complete the shoulder stand. Lie on

70

your back and prop yourself up on your elbows. You should be sitting on top of your hands, with your palms down. Holding this position, arch your back and throw your head back until you feel a stretch under your chin. Hold this position for five complete breathing cycles. Then relax on your back again.

As a variation, you can do the posture with your legs crossed or in a half or full lotus. You'll find that this position makes it easy to take those slow, deep breaths.

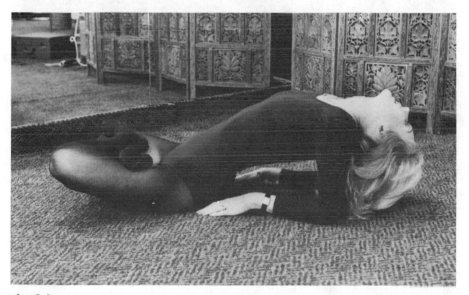

The fish

FORWARD BEND

Sit on the floor with your legs stretched out in front of you. Exhale, and as you inhale, stretch your arms high over your head. Exhale and bend forward slowly. Don't bend your knees, and keep your feet together. Repeat three times for three complete breaths. When you are finished, inhale and rise slowly, then exhale and lower your arms to your sides again. This is a great stretch for the spine, calves, and thighs. It's also a good warm-up or cool-down after running or jogging.

THE TWIST

Sit on the floor with both legs stretched out in front of you. Put your right leg over the left knee and rest your foot on the left side of the knee

Forward bend

The twist

of the extended leg. Then twist your whole body to the right side, making sure that both arms are on the right side of the leg.

Try to keep your left arm against the outside of your right leg for the maximum stretch. Hold this position for three complete breaths. Now repeat the whole twist with the left leg over the right.

THE BOAT

Sit on the floor with your hands at your sides. Stretch your legs out in front. Exhale. Then as you inhale lift your legs together to form a 45-degree angle. Keep your arms extended to the sides of your legs, but do not touch the legs. Hold for five complete breathing cycles and return to the lying position.

The boat

THE RECHARGE

This is a breathing exercise rather than a "position" and is a good way to end the Yoga workout. Sit on the floor in an erect posture—perhaps the *easy posture* or one of the lotus positions. Inhale and exhale a few times through the nose only. Exhale forcefully, pulling in the abdominal

The recharge

muscles as tightly as you can and driving the air out from your lungs. Make sure you do *all* the breathing through the nose. Repeat four or five times, putting all the emphasis on the exhaling motion. The inhalation should be just a fraction of a second.

When you have finished, close your eyes and relax for three complete breathing cycles. Sit quietly in one of the three meditation postures, with your hands resting on your knees.

Dance Movements for Stretching and Limbering

Everybody wants to dance. Just think of the precision footwork of Fred Astaire, the gymnastics of Gene Kelly, Nureyev's classic spins and leaps, or José Greco's staccato heels. Or the new stars, actors who have become dancers, such as John Travolta or Roy Scheider. And who would not be moved by the incredible dynamism of the woman who did Jennifer Beals's dance sequences in the movie *Flashdance?*

Dancing is more popular in the United States now than at any time in its history. We have become a body-conscious culture, and we all want to be able to move our bodies in all the ways that dance provides. We want to be graceful, but we also want to be brassy, quick, and agile. We want to have fluidity of movement, but we also want to be able to do the wild, flaky movements of break dancing.

One of the reasons for the success of *Flashdance* (aside from Ms. Beals's performance) was the sheer energy of the dancing style the movie featured. It was part ballet, part gymnastics, part South-Bronx break dancing, part go-go and strip, and part pure freedom of motion. To see the movie was a liberating experience of the first order.

One of the finest scenes in the movie involved the dancers' workout. They were really pumping iron as well as stretching and jumping and dancing. Dancing is hard work. It doesn't come easy, even to the best, without effort and dedication. Ask any pro.

Even the pros had to start somewhere, so let's begin with some basic movements, basic stretches, basic forms. Let's start with a few classic ballet movements to get you in the spirit of the dance.

GRAND PLIÉ

For this exercise and most of the ones to follow, you'll need either a *barre* (a hip-high wooden or metal bar, attached to a wall) or something to hold on to. If you don't have a barre or a dance studio, a chest top, sofa, or chair back will do.

Stand with your feet together, toes pointing out (you'll feel awkward until you get the hang of it). Now slowly bend your knees, holding on to the barre for balance. You'll notice that your knees are pointing outward if you're doing the motion correctly. Now go down even farther, letting your buttocks drop until you're touching the back of your heels with your hips. Don't "sit" and don't bounce. Rise by pressing your heels down and pushing yourself up with your thighs.

PORT DE BRAS

Stand sideways at the barre—one hand on the barre, the other overhead. Now stretch out and over from the hips, making a huge arc with your body until the whole torso hangs down loosely. Touch your free hand to your toes and come sweeping outward. Your free arm should be overhead. Support the stretch in the torso from the abdominal area.

Now bring yourself up straight again, stretching up and back at the same time. Focus on your hand to keep your balance. Arch your back and stretch. Arch from above the waist and come up waist first. Roll to the center, stretching up and out to avoid swaying your back. Now slide back to the first position (feet together and turned out).

Grand Plié   Port de bras

GRAND BATTEMENT

Begin by facing the barre, with both hands on it. Now slide your right foot along the floor, pointing and stretching until it leaves the floor and

Grand Battement

swings upward. Don't kick—swing it upward and control the movement. The lift should come from the foot, then from the back and inside of the leg. Stretch up on the supporting leg to keep your hips straight (you don't want them to shift). Close by sliding back to first position.

DEVELOPPÉ

Stand facing the barre with your hands on it and your feet in the first position. Now pick up your right foot by pointing the toe and touching it to the heel of the supporting leg. Draw your foot up along the inside of the calf of the supporting leg until your toe touches the knee. Now bring the foot outward and up, keeping the heel forward to maintain the turnout. Extend the leg forward fully so that you feel a good stretch in the inside of the thigh and the back of the knee. Close with both knees straight (try to control the leg until you've lowered it completely).

Developpé

Modern Dance Stretches

Now for a change of pace. Forget the formality and precision of the ballet movements, the French names, and the barre. Now your balance is your own, your movements freer and more improvised. Try these movements from modern dance routines and feel those muscles stretch!

TORSO STRETCH

Sit on the floor—one foot in front of you, the other behind. Sit up straight and raise your arms. Stretch out from the waist—first to the sides, then around and down to the floor in front of you, over to the opposite side, and back up again.

Torso stretch

LOWER ABDOMINAL AND HIP STRETCH

Kneel on the floor on your hands and knees. Keep your back parallel to the floor. Now stretch one leg up and back while you lift your head and throw it back slightly. Next, draw the leg in by contracting the abdominal muscles. Curve your back and tuck your head under. Bring your knee forward to your forehead so that you're curled up into a small ball. Now extend that same leg again, lift your head, and stretch. Return to the starting position and repeat on the other side.

HAMSTRING STRETCH

On the floor, lie flat on your back with your arms down at your sides, palms against the floor. Draw one knee in close to you, touching your forehead with it. Now take hold of the leg just below the calf, holding on

Lower abdominal and hip stretch

Hamstring stretch

with both hands. Extend the leg as far overhead as you can. Feel the stretch in the back of the thigh and the knee. Slowly lower your neck and head to the floor. When the leg is fully extended, let go and slowly lower it to the starting position.

Buttock and thigh stretch

BUTTOCK AND THIGH STRETCH

Lie on your side and raise your top leg about a foot off the floor. Bring the bottom leg up to meet it, then down to the floor again.

WAIST AND TORSO TONER

Stand with the feet about one shoulder-width apart, hands on hips. Lean sideways as far as possible. Then lean forward so that both shoul-

Waist and torso toner

ders are parallel to the floor. In that position, sweep your upper body as far to one side as possible. Then twist your front shoulder so that you're now leaning sideways. Straighten up and repeat for the other side.

LEG STRETCH

Sit on the floor—legs in front of you, knees bent, feet together. Then straighten your left leg out and lift it high, grasping the ankle with both hands. Reverse legs and repeat. Then do the same with both legs raised together, if possible.

Leg stretch

SPINE AND HAMSTRING STRETCH #1

Stand with the legs spread about one shoulder width apart. Grasp one ankle as you bend over and lower your head to the knee of that leg. Switch legs and repeat.

SPINE AND HAMSTRING STRETCH #2

Crouch into a knee bend and grasp your ankles. Then straighten your legs at the knees, coming up slowly. Your ultimate aim is to be able to

Spine and hamstring stretch # 1   **Spine and hamstring stretch # 2**

touch your forehead to your knees. Be careful with this one because it really puts pressure on the lower back.

OVERALL STRETCH

Sit down and tuck one leg under you and extend the other to the side. Then bend over and touch the toes of the extended leg. Straighten up and touch the bent knee (opposite leg) with your opposite hand. Switch legs and repeat.

Overall stretch

THIGH STRETCH

Lift your left (or right) leg up in front of you onto a stool or chair back. Elevate onto your toes and push forward slowly until you feel the stretch in your thighs. Keep your back straight. Return to your original position and repeat with the other leg.

Thigh stretch

Agility and Speed Exercises

Each of the movements described above in the karate, ballet, and modern dance sections can be used to increase your speed and agility. Simply increase the speed at which you do them, keeping your balance and maintaining fluidity of movement at all times. Take several movements in a sequence, and do them without stopping.

For example, you could do a fast series of lateral and front leg raises, combined with an upper back and pectoral stretch and the "ambivalent frog." Or you could combine some of the slow Yoga movements with fast versions of the modern dance movements. Work for gracefulness, fluidity of movement, speed, and timing. Put some slow music on first, then graduate to a fast track.

Okay! Now you're stretched, warmed up, conditioned, and ready for the bodyshaping exercises. Remember that the flexibility exercises in this chapter will help you to avoid injuries and enhance your performance while doing resistance and aerobic exercises. You should always do a warm-up before starting the more strenuous portion of the *Bodysculpture Plus* program, using either the karate, the ballet, or the modern dance stretches. We recommend Yoga for the cool-down after the workout.

Now let's turn to Chapter 5 and a complete set of bodyshaping resistance exercises.

Chapter 5

Resistance Exercises for Bodyshaping, Strength, and Power

Most of the resistance exercises described in this chapter are done with weights: barbells, dumbbells, and various types of exercise machines. You'll find here all the resistance exercises you could ever want, for bodyshaping as well as general fitness, strength, and power. In the program chapter that follows, we'll show you how to combine resistance exercise with aerobics routines for a balanced workout and even faster progress. We'll also show you how to develop your own personalized program to meet your specific needs.

But first you've got to familiarize yourself with the various resistance exercises. To make it easier for you to find the ones you need, there's an index to the exercises in this chapter at the back of the book, beginning on page 196.

Exercises for the Legs

THE SQUAT: GENERAL COMMENTS

This is *the* basic leg exercise. It's usually done with a barbell across the shoulders, although it can be done with the barbell resting in the hands at the top of the chest (this variation is called the "front squat"). If the bar is on the back, make sure it isn't sitting on the neck but is farther down. This way, the trapezius muscles carry the load and you won't injure your neck. If you do front squats, keep your hands close to the center of the bar, with the elbows high and the bar firmly in place at the top of the chest. Make sure that you have enough arm strength to hold it there throughout the exercise movement. Also, balancing will vary, according to the way in which you hold the bar. In any case, be sure you have your feet planted firmly on the floor.

There are four basic ways to do the squat, depending on how far down you go. If you have trouble stretching your Achilles tendons (behind the calf), you will want to place a one-inch-thick wooden block or a book under your heels. In either case, begin the movement with an erect stance, with the back arched, the upper back muscles tensed, eyes straight ahead, and head straight. Grip the bar with both hands, a little more than shoulder-width apart. If you have any doubts about the strength of your lower back, get a lifting belt (see Chapter 1). Tighten the belt before each set of squats, then loosen it between sets.

QUARTER SQUAT

As the name implies, this version of the squat takes you only one-fourth of the way down toward the floor. Do the movement in front of a mirror and you will see how far to go. If you have trouble with your knees, either from lack of strength or from old injuries, try the quarter squat before going on to the other kinds of squats. You will be able to handle considerably more weight in this variation than in the lower-moving squats, but don't become overeager and try it with too much weight (if you do, you may find yourself unable to get back up). When you do squats, always use a spotter (someone to help in case you lose your balance or can't get up).

HALF SQUAT

This one takes you farther down toward the floor than the quarter squat and intensifies the workout of the muscles to the front and to the sides of the thighs. You will feel a hot, flushing sensation in the thighs on about the seventh or eighth repetition if you're doing it right.

PARALLEL SQUAT

This is the most popular squat with both female bodyshapers and male bodybuilders. In this one, you drop slowly until the tops of your

Quarter squat   Half squat

thighs are parallel to the floor. Be careful not to let the back bow forward or you will put undue strain on the lower back. Keep your eyes to the front and your back arched. Keep your lifting belt tight. This exercise provides an intense workout along the full length of the front and outer thigh muscles. When you get to the bottom of the movement, you will also feel the gluteus (hip) muscles come into play.

FULL SQUAT, OR DEEP KNEEBEND

For this one you will certainly need a small book or board under your heels, since you will go all the way down until your buttocks are against your heels. This is the most difficult squat to do, and performing it correctly requires the most strength. It not only works out the front and outer portion of the thigh but the buttocks and the back part of the thigh as well. It taxes your sense of balance, too, and you should be extremely careful to keep your back arched throughout the movement. Think of your entire torso as a curved cylinder that is keeping you together for this one. Keep it all tight.

There is some controversy about the full squat. Many people claim that it is bad for the knees and puts too much strain on both the knees and the back. Granted, if you do the exercise incorrectly and bounce your way from the bottom of the movement halfway back up to a standing position, you certainly will not do your knees any good. Also, if you allow your hips to swing from side to side you will eventually injure your

Parallel squat   Full squat

lower back. On the other hand, if the movement is performed in a slow, deliberate way—not increasing the speed at the bottom of the movement but slowly rising up—you should not suffer any injuries. Remember to keep your back arched! If knee pain or back pain develops, stick with the parallel squat or the half squat and add some lower back exercises to your routine.

THE HACK SQUAT AND THE SISSY SQUAT

The hack squat is usually done on a machine that is especially designed to isolate the muscles of the thigh. If you have access to such a machine, you will readily see how the movement works. Most hack machines are built on sliding rails, and the movement is done by leaning back against the machine, gripping the hand bars, and letting yourself down and up.

Actually, the hack squat is a mechanical variation of the free-weight sissy squat: a form of kneebend pioneered and popularized by West Coast bodybuilding guru Vince Gironda. According to Vince (who has been weight training adviser to Hollywood stars—male and female—for decades), the sissy squat is superior to the regular squat because it puts less strain on the lower back and also makes the legs appear longer than they actually are through the development of the upper thigh muscles.

In the sissy squat, you should hold the bar across the back as in the regular squat, but when lowering your body toward the floor you should keep the upper body in a line perpendicular to the floor. Your buttocks should be slightly tucked in, and your heels should be raised by a block.

This exercise intensifies the leg workout from the knees all the way to the hips. So if you have short legs and want to make them look longer, the sissy squat may do the trick.

Hack squat

Leg extension on a Hydra-Fitness machine

LEG EXTENSION

Now that you've learned how to do various squats, you also need to know about supplemental exercises that will give you the kind of completely rounded development that is a must for any bodyshaping program. The leg extension (or, technically, "extension of the leg at the knee") is an important exercise and can be used in conjunction with the regular squat and sissy squats in supersets (going from one type of squat to the other without rest).

The most popular way to do the leg extension is on a leg-extension machine, such as those built by Hydra-Fitness, Nautilus, or Paramount. But remember, the movement was done 40 years ago, before these machines were even invented. Here's one way of doing the movement without a machine.

Pick up a set of ankle weights at your local sporting goods store. They cost anywhere from $5 to $15 depending on how fancy you want to get. Better yet, look around for a pair of "iron shoes" (cast-iron sandals with leather or cloth straps). These iron shoes will accommodate a dumbbell handle and are thus far more versatile than strap-on ankle weights. You can add weight to the iron shoes all the way to your limit.

If you do the exercise at home with ankle weights or iron shoes, sit down in a chair or on the edge of any sturdy piece of furniture (or on the edge of the porch or stairs). You should put a cushion under your knees to keep your legs from chafing against the surface on which you are sitting. Valerie once wore out the arm of a sofa doing leg extensions with iron shoes. She would sit on a couple of cushions with her legs positioned so that the sofa arm was directly beneath her knees.

The leg extension begins with the knees bent at right angles and the feet hanging down. Raise both legs slowly until they are parallel to the floor. Then lower them back down to the starting position. At the top of the movement, this exercise concentrates on the muscle that locks the knee (the *vastus medius* on the inside of the leg by the knee). If you are flabby in this area, this exercise will tone the muscles as no other can.

LEG CURL

Next on the list of upper leg exercises is the leg curl, which parallels the curls done for the arm biceps. The leg curl isolates the hamstring

Leg curl on a Nautilus machine

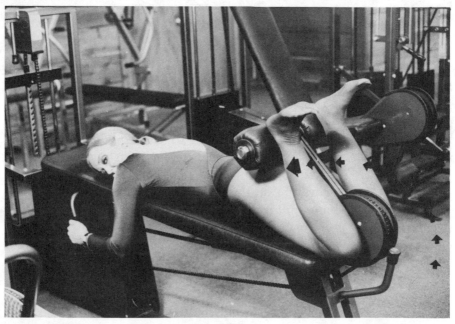

muscles at the back of the upper leg and supplements the workout given to the back of the leg during the full squat. No leg is symmetrical without hamstring development, and the leg curl will give you that flowing contour line that makes for a lean, beautiful look. The exercise can be done with ankle weights or iron shoes. If you belong to a health club, you can do the exercise on a leg curl machine.

The movement begins with the leg extended and ends with the foot pulled up until the heel almost touches the buttocks. If you are working with iron shoes or ankle weights, the greatest intensity can be achieved by doing the movement in a standing position. This way, the tension on the leg biceps is constant and doesn't diminish at the top of the movement. Do the exercise slowly and mechanically. Don't risk injury by jerking the leg up. You can also do this exercise while lying on your stomach, with a friend providing resistance by holding your legs at the ankles.

LEG PRESS

This is a popular leg exercise that works the thighs and hips without the weight of a bar on your shoulders. To work the hips, you must lower the weight all the way down until your knees are against your chest. The

Leg press on a Nautilus machine

only safe way to do this exercise is on a machine. In years past, people actually balanced a barbell on the bottom of their arches and lowered and raised it without a rack or a machine. It gives us goose bumps to think about it! We wonder how many people fell victim to barbells rolling off the feet and onto the neck.

If you do have access to a leg press machine, you should place a pad under your hips to tilt your pelvis up and thus avoid injury to your lower back. *Don't* put your body in an awkward position for this exercise. The weight should traverse an imaginary straight and vertical line from top to bottom. Also remember not to bounce the weight back up from the knees-against-the-chest position. You can break a rib, and you can also sling plates off the machine if it is not pin loaded. The leg press is a terrific exercise, and you should include it in your program, but be careful.

CALF EXERCISES

The calves are the most neglected of all leg muscles. They don't respond to exercise as rapidly as the arms or the thighs, and they also develop a burning sensation during exercise more quickly than any other muscle in the body. The calf muscles are extremely dense and are accustomed to the high-repetition endurance movements that are naturally found in walking, jogging, and running.

Calf raise on a Paramount machine

Moreover, since the calves are ordinarily used almost exclusively for these low-weight, high-rep endurance movements, they are usually lacking in the explosive kind of strength that we associate with the thighs or the arms. It takes a while for them to loosen up and start developing, but persistence will win you a beautiful, shapely set of calves.

There are many ways to do calf exercises, but they all have one thing in common: the heel is raised as high as it will go (this is called "plantar flexion"). Never bounce (you'll pull your Achilles tendon or tear the calf muscle).

Calf raises are done either seated or standing. Standing calf raises seem to concentrate the load on the upper and outer calf muscles (the *gastrocnemius*), while seated calf raises (because of the angle of the knee) seem to concentrate the load on the inner and lower calf muscles (the *soleus*). If your calf lacks development or is flabby at the top, you should concentrate on standing calf raises. If the calf is underdeveloped or flabby just above the ankle, concentrate on seated calf raises.

Whether you do calf raises in a seated or a standing position, certain things remain true of the exercise:

1. To develop the outer portion of the calf, you should do the movement with your toes together and your heels apart.
2. To concentrate on the inner portion of the calf, you should do the movement with your toes pointed outward.
3. To make sure that you develop the entire calf, you should also do additional calf raises with the feet straight or parallel.

In addition, you should do calf raises with the fullest movement possible. Place the toes on a block at least three inches high so that the heel can drop well below the level of the toe at the bottom of the movement. This takes the calf through its entire range of motion and gives it a good, long stretch as well as a good contraction.

Exercises for the Hips and Groin

While men collect fat at the top of the hips, women tend to collect it at the bottom and the sides. A sagging bottom and jodhpur "wings" are the bane of many a woman's existence, and these fat deposits seem to resist any attempt to correct them. When it comes to these areas, a diet is simply not enough, as any veteran Fat Demon fighter will testify. One of the most frustrating experiences in the world is to be in the advanced stages of starvation and have your doctor tell you that your hips are fat because you're not sticking to your diet.

We are also constantly amused and amazed at women's magazine articles that feature hip exercises that have nothing to do with the muscles of the hips. Would that some of the writers (or editors) would take a course in body mechanics or muscular anatomy! And pity the poor woman who takes the articles seriously when they prescribe (for example) standing twists to trim the hips!

Equally distressing are the endlessly reappearing articles that show professional models in shining spandex leotards, lying on the floor flailing their legs or propped up on their shoulders, merrily zipping away on imaginary bicycles. Since no weight is used (much less systematically increased), the body adapts to these cream-puff exercises quickly, with the result that they do no good after about a week.

The hip muscles are many, but the main ones are the glutes—*gluteus maximus* in the rear, *gluteus medius* on the sides—and the various hip flexors that attach to the legs in the front. If you are going to develop that attractive, tight, boxy look about the hips, you've got to put all of these muscle groups through a real workout. Here are some of the best exercises to help you do just that.

FULL SQUAT
(See page 87 for details.) At the very bottom of this lift, most of the work is being done by the glutes. Four intense sets of squats will do more for your sagging bottom than all the imaginary bicycle riding in the world.

STANDING POSTERIOR LEG RAISE
Put on ankle weights or a set of iron shoes. Stand erect, keep your back straight (don't lean forward), and support yourself by grasping a chair, a door frame, or some sturdy object. Slowly swing the leg in an arc to the rear. You won't have a very wide range of motion, so it's best to do the swing slowly in order to derive the maximum benefit from it. Bring the leg slowly back to a point where the feet are side by side. This movement can also be done while lying facedown on the floor. For variety (or if you're traveling), you might want to use a device called a tension band, which is manufactured by the Unique Training Device

| Standing posterior leg raise | Standing front leg raise |

Company (see the manufacturers' list at the back of the book). Tension bands are wide, natural-rubber bands that can be slipped around the legs at the ankles (for maximum tension in the lateral leg raise) or around the knees (for less tension).

STANDING AND RECLINING LATERAL LEG RAISE

See pages 57 and 58. To do these resistance exercises, simply add weight to your feet in the form of ankle weights, iron shoes, or use a tension band.

STANDING FRONT LEG RAISE

Put on ankle weights or iron shoes. Stand erect, bracing yourself with your hands on a doorjamb. Lift the legs alternately, bending the knee slightly as you lift. Bring the knee up as close to the chest as it will go. Don't bow the back or bend forward. Slowly let the leg back down. This exercise will also work the *iliopsoas* muscle group that runs from the inner thighs to the spine.

FRONT LEG RAISE ON A RACK

Many health clubs have leg-raise racks, in which you are supported by your forearms and elbows while your body hangs down between the

Front leg raise on a rack

two armrests. Perform the same motion as described above, but bring both legs up at the same time. This exercise works the abdominal muscles as well as the hip flexors when you raise both legs together. Bend the knees slightly as you raise your legs.

SLANTBOARD LEG RAISE

Lie on your back on a slantboard, reach up behind your head, and grasp the sides of the board. Then raise your legs, knees slightly bent, until they are pointing toward the ceiling at about a 45-degree angle. Use weights as needed.

THE X-RATED HIP EXERCISE

See page 55 for a description of this exercise. To make a resistance exercise out of it, simply have someone sit on your pelvis or hold a barbell plate on your tummy while you do the movement. Don't use much weight at first. Remember that this exercise puts a load on the back as well as the hips.

Exercises for the Waist

The one place where everybody, men as well as women, collect fat is around the waist. We've seen tall, otherwise gorgeously slinky women

Slantboard leg raise

with little pots in front. We've seen naturally fleshy women who have gone completely to fat. Whenever fat collects, it seems to collect first in the waist and specifically in the belly (yes, "belly." If it's flat, you can call it a "tummy," but unsightly, fat-bloated ones are bellies).

As the entire waist collects fat, the belly begins to sag and the fat piles up around the sides, too. Lower backs become broad and are marked by deep creases. Stretch marks also begin to appear as the skin tears because of the load. The most advanced stage of abdominal obesity comes with the appearance of a "fat apron" that hangs halfway down to the knees.

None of this is very pretty, even in a written description. Every woman wants to look trim and sleek, and a flat tummy and squared-off hip tops are a must. Even if you are curvy instead of angular, fat is fat, and any sag at all is too much.

It's poignant to see women in gyms trying to work fat off their bellies. Carl Silvani, the owner of the President and First Lady Health Club in Houston, tells a story about a terrifically overweight woman he observed in his gym one day. She was doing sit-ups like mad—the only exercise she ever did. When he asked her what her goals were, she said she just wanted to get the fat off her waist.

Well, she never did—even when Carl told her that the best way to get the fat off was to combine a strict diet and a total-body workout that

97

includes lots of leg endurance exercises. What was wrong? A number of things. Let's review some of the myths about losing fat around the waist, and you'll see what we mean.

Myth number one: That sit-ups alone will take fat off your waist. No way. Sit-ups don't use enough energy really to burn any fat.

Myth number two: That diet alone will remove the fat from your belly and make it flat. Nope. You have to exercise to get the muscle tone back. A sagging pouch of fat will pull your abdominal muscles downward and add to the overall sag. You have to combine diet *and* exercise.

Myth number three: That sit-ups are the best abdominal exercise. Wrong again. Sit-ups work the abdominals only in the very first part of the movement. They remain clenched until you get almost to the top of the sit-up, but they aren't really worked. Besides, the range of motion of abdominal contraction is actually only a few inches. You don't have to sit all the way up. A crunch will do just fine.

Myth number four: If you concentrate on waist exercises you can burn the fat off the waist first and worry about the rest of the body later. Too bad—and a major myth. Why can't you burn fat segmentally—just from the waist? Because fat is burned systemically, that's why. When more calories are being burned than are being taken in, a signal goes out through the bloodstream to fat that is stored in cells all over the body. The fat is mobilized and taken from these cells to the liver, where it is processed and sent back to muscle cells all over the body to meet energy demands. So you don't burn fat segmentally.

However, although fat burns systemically and not segmentally, perfectly uniform fat mobilization, processing, and burning depends on a perfectly-functioning circulatory system. Unfortunately, nobody has one. Consequently, fat mobilization signals may be interrupted or attenuated (for example, in an area that is saturated with excess fluid); or the circulation from a particular area may be so poor that it prevents easy passage either of the fat-mobilizing signal to the cells or of the mobilized fat to the liver.

Obviously the whole subject of fat burning is extremely controversial. Even among medical doctors there is little agreement about the best way to go about it besides the simple admonition of limiting calories and getting some exercise. Which way to turn? Easy. To the method that works. If you'd really like to learn about the details of the fat-burning process, pick up a copy of our book *Sportspower* (St. Martin's Press, 1983) and you can learn the whole story, from the fat cells to the liver and back again.

So if we can't burn fat segmentally, why do we do waist exercises? Simple. To tone up the waist muscles and get rid of the sag, to increase the circulation in the waist area in order to enhance the removal from the area of excess fluid, mobilized fat, and the by-products of muscle contraction; as well as to strengthen the core muscles (abdominals, obliques, *iliopsoas*, and *lumbarsacral*) that help you stand erect.

RULES FOR GOOD WAIST EXERCISE PERFORMANCE

Although all trainers differ in minor details about how waist exercises are best performed, they all hold some opinions in common. The following is a list of things to remember if you want to get the most out of your waist routine!

1. Concentrate on every movement, whether it's a twist, a crunch, a leg raise, or a side lean. Make each movement count. Focus your concentration the same way you would if you were trying for a new record in the bench press.
2. Vary the movements. Do them slowly with continuous contraction of your muscles one day, then try rapid movements the next. Don't allow your abdominals to adjust to the exercise you're doing.
3. Shake up your waist by adding weight to leg raises or crunches. Try it for a week, then go back to doing them without weights but with more repetitions.
4. Some trainers say that if you work your abdominals every day, you'll smooth out, sag, and never get a flat tummy. Others stoutly maintain that you have to work the abdominals every day. The truth is that different people respond to abdominal exercises in different ways. Try it both ways and then do it the way that works best for you.
5. When you first begin working out with weights, you shouldn't spend an inordinate amount of time on the abdominals. You will find that heavy and endurance leg work in the form of squats, leg presses, and running will do wonders for the abdominals indirectly. Since the legs have the largest muscles in the body, they use a lot of fuel. If you are on a reasonable, balanced, low-calorie diet, solid leg work will help you to peel the fat off your tummy in a hurry.
6. Whatever you do, don't get caught in the trap of thinking that sit-ups and twists will trim the waist if you do them to the exclusion of any

other exercise. Zillions of sit-ups will result in little more than a sore back and a lot of frustration.

These are the fundamental things to remember when doing waist exercises. Now let's learn how to do the exercises themselves.

CRUNCHES
This is a safer, more effective version of the sit-up that is cited by many trainers as being superior to the sit-up in isolating the abdominal muscles. There are several ways to do the exercise.

Crunch with the Knees Raised and Held Together
In this variation, bend the knees and bring them up until the thighs are almost pointing at the ceiling. Raise up until the small of your back is just off the floor and your chin is almost touching your knees. Hold for a count of three and let yourself back down. Do this one on a soft surface, such as a mattress.

Crunch with the Knees Raised and Held Apart
This time keep the knees wide apart and bring yourself up so that your back is just off the floor. Hold for a count of three and let yourself back down.

Crunch with the knees raised and held together

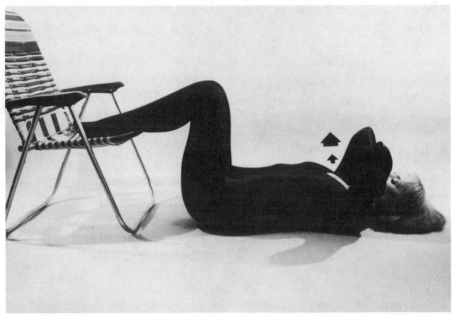

Crunch on a slantboard

Crunch on a Slantboard

Tension on the abdominals is dramatically increased when you do crunches on a slantboard. You should concentrate on flexing the abdominals as you do the movement. The exercise can be done with the knees held together or apart. Be sure that your feet are firmly anchored at the upper end of the slantboard.

Crunch in a Lotus Position

This time put your legs into the traditional Yoga full-lotus position (see Chapter 4, page 64). If you can't do a full lotus, place the knees wide apart and keep the legs crossed at the ankles. Lie back until your body is flat on the floor. As you do the crunch, keep the small of the back against the floor. At the top of the movement, while you are holding the position for a count of three, bring the legs slowly off the floor and pull your pelvis toward your sternum. This will intensify the load on the entire abdominal area.

Side Crunch

This time lie on your side as if you were going to do the reclining lateral leg raises described in Chapter 4. Flex the side muscles (the

Crunch in a lotus position

external obliques) while pulling your legs off the floor. If you are already in good shape, you may be able to bring your upper body off the floor at the same time without pushing up with your arm. Arch your body up to the side as far as you can go and hold for a count of three. Repeat for the requisite number of reps.

SEATED TWIST
See Chapter 4.

Side crunch

BENTOVER TWIST

Holding the bar or broomstick on your shoulders the same way that you would for the seated twist, stand erect, keep your knees straight, and then bend from the waist until your upper body is almost parallel to the floor. Then rotate the body rapidly as far as you can go in either direction. If you do this one correctly, you will feel your sides begin to burn. The faster, the better, once you've warmed up with 10 or 12 reps. Forget about the total number of reps and just time yourself. Do the exercise for about 3 minutes at first and work your way up to 10 minutes.

Bentover twist

SIDE LEAN

This one is no longer as popular as it once was. Some people, both men and women, tend to build side muscles very rapidly, and often the side muscles just make the fat protrude farther. Side leans are still good for strengthbuilding, however, and you should use them if your side muscles are weak.

Stand erect and hold a dumbbell in one hand (don't use two dumbbells or they will counterbalance each other and cancel out the effort required to make the lift). Place the other hand on the hips. Lean toward the side where the dumbbell is being held. Go down as far as you can. Maintain a strict sideways movement. Don't allow yourself to bend forward. Do the requisite number of reps, then try it with the other hand and the other side. See Chapter 4, for a version without weights.

SIDE LEAN VARIATION

If you want to work the muscles to the sides and the back of the waist directly over the hip bones, follow your regular side leans with another set, this time with a lean that is about 45 degrees to the front. You'll feel the difference.

BACK CRUNCH OR SPINAL HYPEREXTENSION

Lie on the floor facedown and extend your arms past your head until the elbows are completely straight. Your legs should also be straight, with the knees locked. Then arch your back and lift both the arms and legs off the floor. Don't just bend the arms and the legs at the shoulders and the hips. Let the back arch itself do the lifting so that the work will be concentrated on the small of the back.

Side lean

Side lean variation

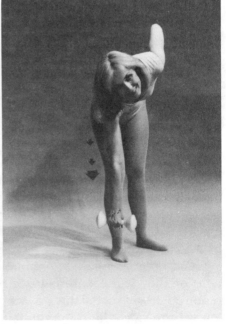

Back crunch or spinal hyperextension

BACK CRUNCH OR SPINAL HYPEREXTENSION
ON A ROMAN BENCH

Many health clubs feature a piece of equipment called a Roman bench, which itself is a modern version of the old Roman chair (supposedly invented in ancient Rome), which was a sit-up intensifier. The Roman bench has a pad on which you can lie, facedown, with your pelvis across the pad. The backs of your calves will hook under a padded horizontal bar.

Put your arms behind you, pull your shoulders back with your elbows locked and your hands clenched together (this will help keep the spine straight). Bend at the waist and let your body dip slightly below an imaginary line that is parallel to the floor. Then arch your back up as far as you can and hold for a count of three.

FRONT LEG RAISE (add ankle weights for resistance)

See Chapter 4 and this chapter for details.

VERTICAL LEG RAISE ON A RACK

See this chapter for details.

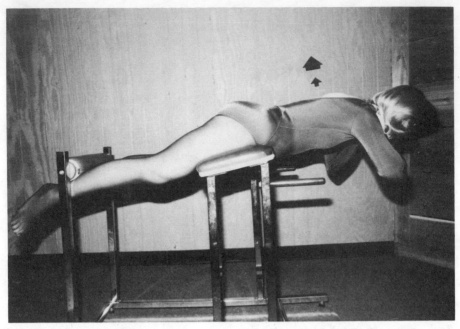
Back crunch or spinal hyperextension on a Roman bench

LEG RAISE ON A SLANTBOARD
See this chapter for details.

STIFF-LEGGED DEADWEIGHT LIFT
This is an injury-prone exercise, and although it is still included in many programs, we no longer recommend it and do not include it in this book.

REGULAR DEADWEIGHT LIFT
The regular deadweight lift is used by almost everybody who wants to build strength in the lower back. The lift combines the effort of the arms, shoulders, upper, middle, and lower back muscles, plus the legs and hips. The forearms also get a workout from the effort required to hold on to the bar. It is also one of the three lifts required in competition power lifting. You can use it either to make your lower back more shapely and trim or to make your lower back strong and powerful. It all depends on how hard you want to work.

This exercise begins with a barbell lying in front of you on the floor. Stand erect, then bend the legs at the knees and drop down to grasp the bar with the hands about 18 inches apart. Keep the buttocks low and

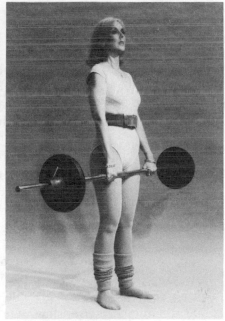

Regular deadweight lift
(starting position)

(end of movement)

really bend the knees. Your knees should be between your arms (regular style) or spread wide to the outside of your arms (sumo style). Try them both to see which is more comfortable for you.

At the start of the lift, your back should be parallel to the floor. As you lift the bar, do most of the work with your legs, otherwise you'll strain your lower back. Stand erect in one fluid movement and arch your back at the top of the lift. Then lower the barbell back down to the floor, bending your knees and your back simultaneously.

Exercises for the Middle and Upper Back

The upper and middle back are made up of two major muscle groups, the latissimus dorsi (or "lats") and the trapezius (or "traps"). If you have underdeveloped traps, you will be bony and coat hangerish along the shoulders and your shoulderblades will stick out like vestigial wings. If you have underdeveloped lats, from behind you will appear larger at your waist than at the point directly under the arms. Don't neglect either of these two important muscle groups.

All of the middle and upper back exercises can be done at home with free weights. However, many are best done with cables and pulleys. With a little ingenuity, anbody can build a pulley machine at home. All that's needed is a length of cable (preferably coated with vinyl for smoothness and durability), a handle to hold on to, a heavy-duty pulley (you can get them at your neighborhood hardware store), a couple of long eyebolts and a couple of nuts and washers, and something sturdy to hang the pulley hook on.

If you belong to a health club, there will undoubtedly be a pulley machine available. Here are a few tips on the proper use of pulley machines:

1. Make sure you have a firm grip on the bar or handle before you start the exercise. If you let it slip out of your hands, the weights at the other end of the cable will come down with a crash.
2. Do all pulley exercises slowly and deliberately. Jerking on the handle may cause cable breakage.
3. Be sure that you go through the entire possible range of motion. Don't cheat on the movements.
4. When you reach the point in overhead pulley work where you are lifting a weight close to your own bodyweight, you may have to have a friend hold you down as you do the lift.
5. If you're using a pin-loaded machine, be sure the pin is securely positioned in its hole. Otherwise the whole stack of weights may fall while you're in the middle of your lift.
6. Some pulley bars or handles are straight, and others are bent. Still others allow you to hold your hands with the palms facing. Some have rubber grips and others have knurling (crisscrossed grooves cut into the metal). You may want to wear lifting gloves to protect your hands.

Got the picture? Now here are the exercises.

LATISSIMUS EXERCISES

Pulldown Behind the Neck
Grasp the bar in both hands with a wide grip, palms facing away from you. Sit down on the floor and pull the bar down until it's touching the area just behind your neck. Keep your legs either crossed or extended in front of you. Slowly raise the bar back up until your arms are straight.

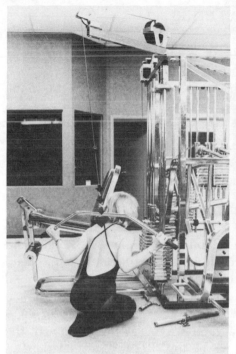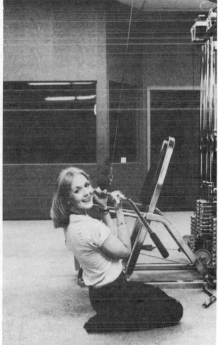

Pulldown behind the neck   Pulldown to the chest

Pulldown to the Chest

Grasp the bar at its center with both hands touching at the heel of the hands, palms facing you. Sit down cross-legged on the floor and pull the bar down to the chest just under the chin. Arch the back as you pull down. Then slowly raise the bar back up until the arms are straight.

Two-Arm Bentover Rowing

This exercise is done with a barbell instead of pulleys. It is a controversial exercise since it is easy to injure the lower back if the exercise is not done in strict form. You should *never* jerk the weight up when doing bent over rowing, and you should never use so much weight that the only way you can get it to the chest is by jerking it. The main thing to remember is to keep the back arched. Most people let the back bow like that of a frightened cat when they do this exercise. This means that the back is in its weakest configuration. Keep the back arched, with the muscles along the spine tensed at all times.

The exercise begins with a barbell lying in front of you. Bend down and grasp the barbell with both hands, with a grip little more than shoulder-width apart, palms facing downward. Keep the knees slightly bent, keep the back arched, and the body bent at the waist (but never more than 45 degrees). Pull the barbell up until it is almost touching a point just below the breastbone. The elbows should be kept close to the sides. This will concentrate the load on the latissimus muscles. If you want to shift the load to the upper back, keep the arms straight and retract or pull back your shoulders.

One-Arm Bentover Rowing

In this exercise you will use a dumbbell instead of a barbell. Place your feet about shoulder-width apart and lean at the waist toward the floor until your upper body is almost parallel to the floor. Rest one hand on a bench for balance and grasp a dumbbell with the other hand. Keep the elbows of the lifting arm close to your side and bring the dumbbell up until it is even with the side of your waist. Then slowly return it to the starting position.

Practice this lift until you feel a good stretch at the bottom of the movement and a good contraction at the top. Because of variations in individual structure you will have to find the right "groove" that does the most for you. This is an excellent exercise for the lower lats, but you

Two-arm bentover rowing

One-arm bentover rowing

must concentrate on letting the lats do the movement instead of the arms. Think of your hands merely as hooks and your arms merely as inanimate pieces of wood that connect the hooks to the lats.

TRAPEZIUS EXERCISES

Now let's move up to the upper back. The trapezius muscles give your shoulders that trim, lean look that makes it easy to hold up your head and look young. For many women a combination of fat, weak trapezius, and neck muscles gradually make their chins jut out, their heads sag, their necks angle to the front, and their shoulders droop.

When the shoulders droop, the chest becomes concave and the bust disappears. A sagging upper body also tends to thrust the pelvis to the front, tucking the bottom in and making it disappear. The entire body becomes a sagging slouch of angles instead of a slender system of gentle arcs. We've already covered the lower back. Here are the upper back exercises you need for better posture and a more vital look.

Shoulder Shrug with Dumbbells

Grasp a dumbbell in each hand; stand erect, with your back straight and your shoulders slumped forward. Hold the dumbbells to the front and sides of your legs, with their handles forming a triangle in front of you. Pull your shoulders up and back, arching your lower back and lifting and rotating the shoulders as high and as far back as they will go. Then slowly release the tension and let your shoulders slump back down to the starting position. Don't let the arms bend at the elbows. This is a traps exercise not an arm exercise.

Shoulder Shrug with a Barbell

This variation is done in essentially the same way as the dumbbell shrugs, but this time you will use a barbell. Grasp the bar with your hands about 18 inches apart. Keep your arms straight, with the palms facing your groin. Lift upward and backward, rotating the shoulders as you go.

Upright Rowing with a Low Pulley

This exercise works the shoulders as well as the traps. Sit on the floor facing a low-pulley station. Grasp the bar with your hands about 3 to 4

Shoulder shrug with dumbbells   **Shoulder shrug with a barbell**

Upright rowing with a low pulley

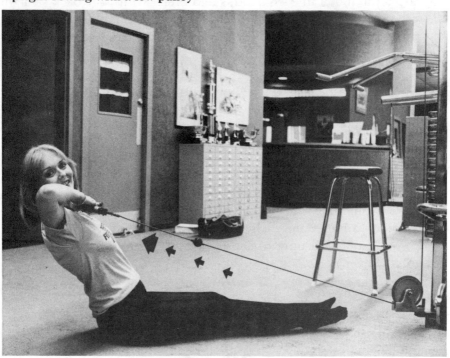

112

inches apart, palms facing you. Lean back, back straight or slightly arched, and pull the bar in a straight line from the front of your thighs to a point in front of your chin. At the top of the movement, try to lift the bar a little past the level of your chin, and you will feel the traps come into play. Keep your elbows high as you pull the bar.

Exercises for the Chest

The chest is made up of the pectoral muscles, which lie under the breasts and span the area from the center of the breastbone to the shoulders and from the collarbone to the sternum. The breasts themselves, of course, are composed of mammary glands and a cushion of fat. It is the fat not the glands that disappears when you go on a strict diet and exercise program.

Chest exercises develop the pectoral muscles; they do not increase the size of the mammary glands that make up the breasts. However, pectoral exercises *will* make your breasts firmer and provide the muscular foundation needed to give them a lift. Lack of pectoral development will result in sagging breasts, just as lack of abdominal development leads to a sagging tummy.

Don't be dismayed if your breasts seem to diminish in size with diet and exercise. You're only losing the fat. And beneath the breasts you're replacing the fat with good, strong, taut muscle. Further, as Dr. Barbara Edelstein has pointed out, once you've lost the fat you're going to lose, fat will redistribute itself around the body. Which means that what you seemed to have lost, you will get back—but this time it will be shapelier, firmer, and higher. Valerie went through a period when her bust seemed to disappear almost completely only to return three months later greatly improved. So do your chest exercises and don't spare the effort.

THE BENCH PRESS: A FEW TIPS
BEFORE YOU START LIFTING

This is by far the most popular of all weight-training lifts. It involves the pectoral muscles of the chest as well as the muscles of the shoulders and upper arms. It will expand your rib cage, firm up your bust, get rid of unsightly collarbones, trim down flab on the underside of your upper arms, and make you stronger than you ever thought possible.

A few words of warning are in order, however, before we begin our description of the bench press:

1. Never do the bench press without a spotter or workout partner. Every year we see a few people injured in this lift when they can't get the bar back up that last time. Have somebody there to get the bar off your chest (or neck) if your arms give out.
2. If you're foolish enough to do the bench press without a spotter and you wind up with the bar across your chest and no strength in your arms to get it off, don't panic. Keep both hands on the bar and use every ounce of energy you've got to roll it toward your abdomen while lunging up in a sit-up. This usually works, but it can be painful, especially for a woman.
3. Make sure you have a tight grip on the bar. Use an opposing-thumb grip, just as you would use if you were picking up a glass of water. In years past, it was popular to grip the bar with the fingers and the thumbs on the same side of the bar. You may still see some people around the gym using this grip. Avoid it. The bar can easily slip out of your hands, roll across your wrist, and fall on your neck or chest.
4. If you want to put the load primarily on the pectoral muscles, use a wide grip with the hands about two feet wider than shoulder-width apart. A narrow grip, on the other hand, shifts the load to the arms and the anterior deltoids (the front shoulder muscles).
5. Many health clubs provide Olympic-style or power-lifting bars. If you use one of these bars, be aware that the bar and collars (without any plates) weigh 55 pounds. The smaller bars that you would probably buy for a home barbell set weigh only 15 to 25 pounds. So don't get into trouble by miscalculating the weight of an Olympic bar.
6. Olympic and power-lifting bars also often have deep knurling for a surer grip. You may want to wear lifting gloves to protect your hands when using one of these bars.
7. Make sure you have the same amount of weight on both ends of the bar. It's also a good idea to use collars, to keep plates from sliding off if you raise one arm faster than the other. Finally, make sure your hands are positioned equidistant from the center of the bar in order to equalize the load on both arms and make it possible for you to keep your balance.
8. Make sure that this lift is done on a narrow bench so that the elbows can come down past the line of the body. Otherwise you would not be able to lower the bar all the way to the chest. If you don't have a bench-press rack (which has metal hooks on which the barbell rests), you'll have to have a spotter to hand you the weight and then take it from you when you finish the exercise.

9. When you take the barbell off the rack hooks, lift it upward until it is above your chest. Then slowly lower the barbell until it lightly touches your chest. Without stopping at the bottom of the lift, push your arms upward until the barbell is again at arms' length.

10. Each person does the bench press in a slightly different way due to differences in bone structure and musculature. Experiment with different grip widths and also lower the barbell to different places on the chest until you find your own groove. For example, Valerie does best with a moderately wide grip, lowering the bar to the top of the chest. Ralph does best with a wide grip, lowering the bar to the middle of the chest.

11. The bench press is what is called a compound lift. That is, it involves several muscle groups, all working in unison. You should therefore do 8 to 10 warm-up repetitions with a light weight before going on to the regular exercise weight. This will prevent muscle pulls and elbow injuries.

It all sounds very complicated, doesn't it? And a little bit dangerous. We hope we haven't scared you away from the bench press with this long list of concerns. The bench press is one of the most important exercises in this book, but we don't want you to get hurt doing it. Once you get it sorted out, you'll love it. It's our favorite exercise.

The bench press has three basic variations, as follows.

Regular Bench Press

Lie on your back on a bench. Reach up and grip the bar with both hands (either wide grip for more chest work or narrow grip for more arm work). Lift the bar off the rack hooks, straighten the arms, then lower the barbell to the chest. Don't stop, but with a fluid movement reverse the direction of the barbell and extend the arms up toward the ceiling. When you have done the requisite number of repetitions, place the barbell back on the rack hooks.

Incline Bench Press

This version is done on an incline bench. The purpose is to shift the load to the upper pectorals. If you have a sagging bustline, this is the exercise for you. Some health clubs have machines that will enable you to do this exercise without a spotter. Otherwise you'll need a workout partner. The best way to do the exercise is not with a machine but with

 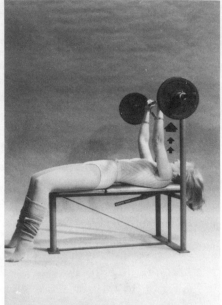

Regular bench press   **(end of movement)**
(lowered position)

an incline bench-press rack. An incline bench is slid under the rack and the barbell is placed on the rack hooks just as in the regular bench press. Lie back on the incline bench, reach up, and grasp the bar. Lift it off the rack hooks and lower it until it reaches a point at the top of the chest. Extend the arms straight toward the ceiling until the elbows are straight, using a wide grip for pectoral work and a narrow grip for arms and shoulders.

Decline Bench Press

The decline bench press shifts the load to the lower pectorals. You'll need a special bench for this one—one that will allow you to lie with your head toward the floor and your feet toward the ceiling. The movement is still the same: grasp the bar, lift it off the rack hooks, and lower it to the chest (this time to a point at the bottom of the breastbone or sternum). Straighten the arms toward the ceiling. Put the barbell back on the rack when you've done the requisite number of reps.

Partial Bench-Press Movements

If you are weak at the bottom of the lift (when the bar is close to the chest), you should do extra work to strengthen the pectorals. Take the bar off the rack the usual way, lower it until it touches the chest, then lift

116

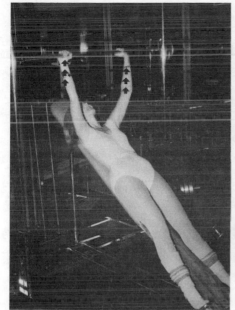 

Incline bench press   Decline bench press

it only about 6 or 7 inches before lowering it again. Use a very wide grip and a light weight at first. After about 10 reps, your pectorals should begin to get warm and feel full.

If you are weak at the top of the lift, when the arms are almost fully extended, you should do partial movements with a moderate grip, lowering the bar only about 6 to 7 inches. Again, start with a light weight and build up to heavier lifts.

You can do partial movements with regular, incline, or decline bench presses. The goal here is to be able to do the lift with a fluid movement. The pectorals and anterior deltoids do most of the work at the bottom of the lift, and the arms take over as they extend toward the ceiling. If you are stronger in the pectorals and deltoids, you will be able to handle more weight at the bottom of the lift than at the top. If you are stronger in the arms, the situation is reversed.

FLYES

The bench press is not the only pectoral exercise, although its popularity tends to turn attention away from the others. The "flye" (the name is a linguistic barbarism, derived from "flying exercise") is the second most popular chest exercise. There are basically two ways to do flyes—straight-arm and bent-arm—each working the pectorals in a slightly different way. They can also be done on a regular horizontal bench or on an incline or a decline bench. The incline bench version works the

117

upper pectorals, the decline works the lower pectorals, and the horizontal bench works the entire pectoral group.

Straight-Arm Flye

In this version hoist two dumbbells to a position above the chest, arms fully extended, while you are lying on your back. Bring the dumbbells down to the sides in an arc that is perpendicular to the body, stopping when the arms are almost parallel to the floor. Then bring the arms slowly back to the starting position. Although it is called a straight-arm flye, you should bend your elbows slightly to avoid injury. Use a very light weight at the beginning.

Bent-Arm Flye

Begin as above but bend the elbows at a little more than a 45-degree angle. Since the elbows are bent, you can bring the upper arms down past the plane of your body and thus get a fuller range of motion in the lift. When you've lowered the arms as far as they will go, slowly raise them back to the starting position.

Straight-arm flye

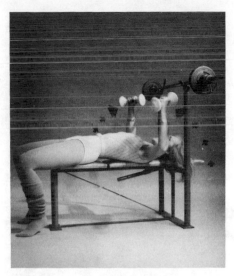

Bent-arm flye

Hand Positions for Flyes

Two hand positions are used in doing flyes. You may start (with the arms extended toward the ceiling) with the palms facing each other or facing your feet. Another way to do flyes is to start with the palms facing each other at the top of the lift and rotate the forearms during the lift so that the palms are facing your feet when your arms are down at your sides. If the palms are facing throughout the lift, the biceps help to stabilize the arms during the lift. If the forearms are rotated or if the palms are kept facing your feet, the stability function is shifted to the *brachialis* muscles. These muscles run along the outside of the biceps and are weaker than the biceps. Thus flyes are harder if you do them with the palms facing the feet. Do them both ways for balanced development.

PULLOVERS

Another compound exercise that benefits the chest is the pullover. There are several ways to do it, and it not only works the pectorals but the latissimus and *serratus* muscles under the arms as well. Pullovers are a good chest expander if you breathe properly during the movement. Do them slowly and deliberately.

Straight-Arm Pullover

Lie on a bench either lengthwise or crosswise so that your shoulders are firmly supported by the bench and your back is arched, knees bent at a 90-degree angle, and the feet firmly planted on the floor. Grasp a

119

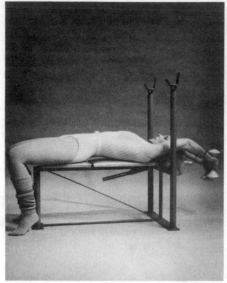 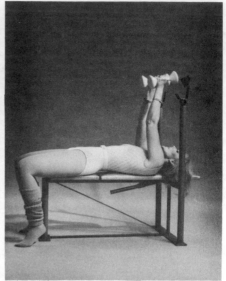

Straight-arm pullover   (end of movement)
(starting position)

dumbbell not by the handle but under the plates at one end. Make sure the plates are securely fastened—you don't want the dumbbell coming apart in your face!

Extend your arms toward the ceiling until the elbows are only slightly bent. Take as deep a breath as you can and lower the dumbbell in an arc until it is below the plane of your body past the top of your head. Then slowly raise the dumbbell back to the starting position while exhaling. As you do this lift, experiment with different elbow positions. You'll find that by varying the angle at the elbow slightly, you can shift the load back and forth between the latissimus and the pectoral muscles. The abdominals should be contracted during this exercise, especially as you raise the dumbbell. You won't need much weight on this lift, especially at the beginning. Breathe deeply!

Bent-Arm Pullover

In this version the breathing cycle remains the same and the weight is held in the same way. However, here you should bend your arms at the elbows as you lower the weight so that the elbows form almost a 90-degree angle at the bottom of the movement. As you bring the arms back up, decrease the angle of the forearms to about 45 degrees. At the top of the lift the arms should be straight again. You can handle a great deal more weight with the arms bent, but don't get carried away with poundages. This exercise is primarily a chest expander and a supplement to the bench press. Breathe deeply!

120

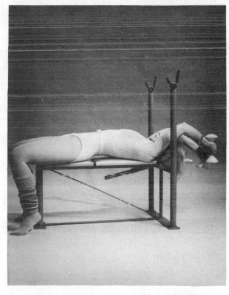

Bent-arm pullover
(starting position;
end of movement is same as
in straight-arm pullover)

PULLEY PULLOVERS

You can also use a pulley machine for pullovers. Most health clubs have overhead pulleys for latissimus exercises, and these can easily be adapted to pullover work. Simply set the weight-selection pin for a light weight, slide an incline bench under the overhead pulley, lie back on

Pulley pullover

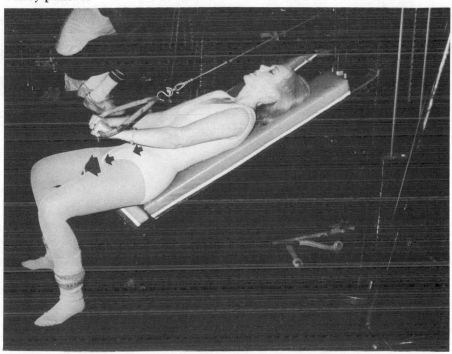

the bench, grasp the pulley handle, and perform the exercise. You can do it either straight-arm or bent-arm.

If there is no overhead pulley available, you can also do this exercise on the low pulley. Lie on your back on the floor with your head toward the low pulley. Reach past your head and grasp the bar. As you bring your arms over your head, be careful and don't get your hair tangled in the pulley cable.

Exercises for the Shoulders

The shoulders are made up of the *deltoid* muscles, which are divided into 3 sections, the *anterior* muscles (to the front), the *medial* or *lateral* muscles (to the sides) and the *posterior* muscles (to the back). While many of the shoulder exercises are done with dumbbells, the basic ones are done with a barbell. The shoulder muscles lift the arms to the front, to the sides, or to the rear.

If you tend to look like a coat hanger, underdeveloped deltoids are probably the reason. On the other hand, if you are overweight, under-developed shoulders translate into rounded shoulders and forward droop. No active woman should neglect her shoulders just because not much fat is stored there. You can't have beautiful neck/shoulder/upper arm contours with weak or underdeveloped deltoids.

To make your shoulders look their best, you should be sure to work all three heads of the deltoids. Following are all the exercises you'll need:

BENCH PRESS (for the anterior and lateral deltoids)
See "Regular Bench Press" above.

MILITARY PRESS
One of the oldest standbys in weight training is the military press (so named because of the erect posture held during the lift). The military press used to be one of three Olympic competition lifts, but it was abandoned because lifters were injuring their backs by bending too much during record attempts.

The military press started, however, as a basic compound arm/shoulder exercise, to work the triceps (the back of the arm) and the anterior and lateral deltoid muscles. Here's how to do it.

Stand erect with your feet a little more than shoulder-width apart.

 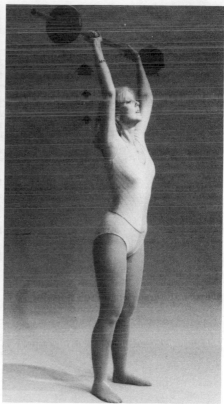

Military press (starting position)   **(end of movement)**

Bend at the waist and the knees and grasp a barbell with the hands about shoulder-width apart. Lift the barbell from the floor to a position at the top of the chest and pause for a moment. Then, without arching your back unduly, push the barbell overhead until your arms are straight. When the lift is completed the barbell will be in a position above and slightly behind your head. Return the barbell to the top of your chest and repeat the lift.

SEATED PRESS (for the front and lateral deltoids)

This variation of the military press avoids some of the danger of back injuries. It can be done behind the neck, in front of the chest, or alternating between the two positions. Here goes:

Seated Press from the Chest

Follow the same procedure as above but position the barbell to be lifted at the top of your chest, as if you were going to do a front squat

 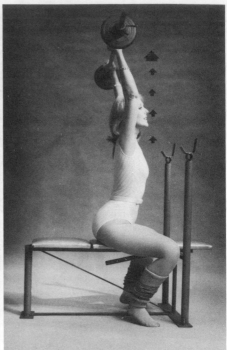

Seated press from the chest   **(end of movement)**
(starting position)

with it. Push the barbell overhead in the same manner as you would if you were doing the standing military press. Lower and repeat.

Seated Alternating Partial Press

If you want to work the deltoids at different angles during the same exercise, combine the behind-the-neck and the seated chest press. Start off with the barbell behind the neck. Lift it up (but only a few inches above the head), then lower it to a position at the top of the chest. Lift it up and lower it back behind the press. Continue for several repetitions, alternating the starting point each time. Don't lean the head from side to side as you do the lifts, and don't straighten the arms completely.

ANTERIOR RAISE (primarily for the anterior deltoids)

Stand erect with either a barbell or two dumbbells held in your hands, palms facing you, arms straight, weight resting in front of the thighs. Slowly raise the weight in an arc to the front until it is almost overhead, but don't carry the movement to the point where tension is taken off the deltoids. Don't swing the weight up, but lift it slowly.

When you reach the top of the movement, slowly lower the weight to

124

the starting position. You should keep your arms almost straight, with the elbows slightly bent. If this exercise is done with dumbbells, you should alternate arms, lifting first the right and then the left in an arc.

Anterior raise   Lateral raise

LATERAL RAISE (primarily for the lateral deltoids)

Stand erect, holding a dumbbell in each hand. The dumbbells should be positioned in front of the thighs, and your palms should be facing each other. Lift the two dumbbells at the same time, making an arc to the sides and slightly to the back until the arms make about a 45-degree angle with the floor. If you do this one correctly, you'll find that it is physically impossible to lift the arms all the way overhead.

Many people continue the arc overhead by shifting their balance and rotating their shoulders so that the anterior deltoids complete the lift. This is unnecessary. There is a diminishing load on the shoulders once the arms have passed the horizontal plane. There is no need to go higher. Instead, lean slightly forward during the lift and raise the arms up and back until they reach a natural locking position.

POSTERIOR RAISE

Stand erect, then bend at the waist until your upper body is almost parallel to the floor. Arch your back and keep it arched. Reach down and

Posterior raise

grasp a dumbbell in each hand. Lift the dumbbells to the sides in an arc that ends with the arms above the plane of the bentover upper body.

POSTERIOR RAISE ON AN INCLINE BENCH

Grasp a dumbbell in each hand and carefully lie facedown on an incline bench. Let your arms hang down on either side of the bench. Raise your head and arch your back. Then lift the dumbbells in an arc to the sides until they are above the level of your shoulders. Don't swing them toward your feet.

Exercises for the Arms

Few women ever think about building strength in their arms other than the strength needed to play tennis or golf, to swim, or to participate in what have always been considered "women's" sports. The new, active, modern American woman, however, wants total-body strength for a wide variety of activities ranging from skydiving to the martial arts. Unfortunately, women neglect their arms even in health clubs where there are machines designed especially for arm development.

Don't make this mistake. If the front of your upper arms are flabby, it's probably as much from underdeveloped biceps as from fat. The same goes for the triceps in the back of the upper arm. And don't worry about building bulging biceps. As we'll show you in the program chapter, if you had any idea how many hundreds of hours of intense effort is required for women to build any appreciable muscle size at all, you would know that there is absolutely no danger of your looking like a muscle-man. Besides, what most women interpret as growing arm muscles are actually already-existing muscularity finally being uncovered from cushions of fat.

In addition, arm exercises are fun to do and don't involve nearly the effort that heavy leg work does. You may find yourself looking forward to arm day at the gym! Let's start with the biceps and work our way around the arms.

EXERCISES FOR THE FRONT OF THE UPPER ARM

Two-Arm Curl with a Barbell

This is another old favorite. It used to be called the "military curl" for the same reasons of posture as the military press. Stand erect, holding a barbell at arms' length in front of you, resting across the tops of your thighs, palms to the front. Keep your elbows at your sides and slowly lift the barbell in an arc until it is at a position about 9 inches from your chin. Don't let it "fall into" your chest at the top of the movement—this will only take the tension off the biceps and lessen the effectiveness of the exercise. Slowly lower the arms down to the starting position and repeat the movement.

Curl with Dumbbells

Curls can also be done with dumbbells. The position is the same as for the barbell curl above. You will find that you will not be able to use as much weight with dumbbells as with a barbell because you will also have to be concerned with keeping the dumbbells going in the right direction.

For this reason, dumbbell curls also work out the auxiliary muscles (the ones that are indirectly involved in making a lift by keeping your body aligned or by supporting the muscles that are doing the actual lifting). In this case, the trapezius and shoulders are also getting a workout.

 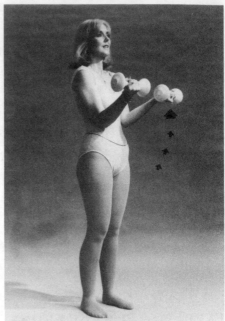

Two-arm curl with a barbell   Curl with dumbbells

In addition, you can do dumbbell curls either together or alternating. That is, you can either bring both arms up at the same time or in sequence. Either way, you'll get a good biceps workout.

Concentrated Curl

For this one, sit down on a bench with your knees about a foot apart and your feet firmly planted on the floor. A dumbbell should be between your feet. Brace your right elbow against the inside of your right leg at the knee and grasp the dumbbell in your right hand. Using your right leg to prevent your elbow from moving backward, lift the dumbbell in a curling motion. This movement isolates the biceps, thus concentrating the load on the biceps alone.

Reverse Curl

The biceps aren't the only muscles involved in curls. The brachialis runs along the outside of the biceps and also helps flex the arm at the elbow, either more or less, depending on the position of the hand. Let us explain. Hold your hand up in front of you, with the palm facing you. Your hand is now in a supinated position. Now rotate your forearm so that the palm is away from you. Your hand is now in a pronated position.

When you do curls with the hands supinated, the biceps do most of the work. When curls are done with the hands pronated, the brachialis

Concentrated curl   Reverse curl

does most of the work. Curls done with the hands pronated are called reverse curls. These curls are done exactly the same as the regular curls but with a different hand position.

Pulley Work for the Biceps

Additional work for the biceps can be done on pulley machines. Just grasp the pulley bar and pull it toward you. If you immobilize your elbows, you can get the effect of a concentrated curl.

Supinating Curl

Any of the dumbbell curls described above can also be converted into what is called a supinating curl. Start the movement with the hands pronated and rotate your forearms as you bring the weight up. The hands should be fully supinated at the top of the lift.

That takes care of the front of the upper arm, now let's turn to the triceps in the back of the arm.

EXERCISES FOR THE BACK OF THE UPPER ARM

The triceps make up two thirds of the upper arm's mass. They are used in any arm movement that involves pushing away from your body.

Pulley work for the biceps

Underdeveloped triceps yield "stick figure" arms that are best kept under long sleeves. If you want to give your arms the natural contour that shows them at their best, triceps exercises are a must. Here are the best.

**Supinating curl
(starting position)**   **(hand rotates in
middle of movement)**   **(end of movement)**

Bench Press
See pages 113 to 115.

Incline Bench Press
See pages 115 and 116.

Decline Bench Press
See page 116.

Military Press
See pages 122 and 123.

Seated Press
See pages 123 and 124.

Triceps Extensions: Comments
Triceps extensions involve extending the arm at the elbow—that is, starting with the elbow bent and ending the lift with the arm straightened. The exercise isolates the triceps and really gives them a workout. These exercises used to be called French curls, although we have never found anyone who knew why. There are several ways to do them. The following are the most effective forms of the exercise:

Seated Triceps Extension
Sit on a bench, preferably with your back braced, holding a dumbbell in your right hand. Raise the dumbbell overhead. Keep the upper arm pointing toward the ceiling, bend the arm at the elbow, and lower the dumbbell in an arc until it is beside your head. Then push the dumbbell up in an arc toward the ceiling until the arm is fully extended overhead again. Repeat with the other arm. This exercise can be done with a barbell, working both arms at the same time. Make sure that your hands are in the center of the barbell. Grip the bar with your hands close to each other.

Seated triceps extension   Kickback

Standing Triceps Extension

Exactly the same as above but in a standing position. A barbell can be used instead of a dumbbell.

Reclining Triceps Extension

Lie on your back on a bench, holding a dumbbell above your body at arms' length by the underside of the plates instead of the handle (the same way you held it for the pullovers on pages 119 and 120). Lower the dumbbell in an arc until it is in a position right above the top of your head. A barbell can be used in this one, too. Don't hit yourself on the top of the head with the weight.

Kickback

Bend at the waist until the upper body is parallel to the floor. Grasp a dumbbell with the right hand and brace your left forearm against your left leg. Keep the right elbow against the body with the upper arm parallel to the body. Lift (don't swing) the dumbbell in an arc to the back until the arm is straight. Slowly lower it to the starting position.

132

EXERCISES FOR THE FOREARMS

The muscles of the forearms, along with the calves, are among the most neglected in the body. We work them indirectly every time we play tennis or drive a car, lift a glass or wave a hand. Few of us exercise them deliberately or systematically. Because women rarely train their upper bodies or arms for strength, their forearms are usually weak. In some cases the weakness prevents the use of an effective amount of weight in other exercises. If you can't hold on to it, you can't lift it!

The following exercises will strengthen the forearms and help you to develop more strength in your hands:

Wrist Flexion

Hold a dumbbell in your hand with the palm up. Sit in a chair, bend over, and rest your forearm along your thigh. Let your hand dangle over the edge of your knee. Now raise your hand as far as you can raise it while keeping your wrist firmly placed at your knee. Do both arms.

Radial Flexion

Assume the same position as above but with the hands turned palms facing each other, holding light dumbbells. Lift the hands upward at the wrists without moving the rest of the arms.

Wrist flexion (starting position)   **(end of movement)**

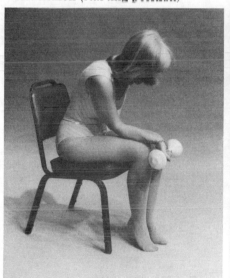

Radial flexion (starting position)   **(end of movement)**

Now you have all the exercises. Let's move on to the program chapter, where we'll put them all together in a systematic set of routines for weight loss, bodyshaping, strength, speed, agility, and endurance.

Chapter 6

Bodysculpture Plus Personalized Programs

In Chapter 3 we cited as a fundamental principle of exercise physiology the fact that each kind of exercise is "specific." Thus aerobic exercises will condition the cardiovascular system and give you endurance, but they won't help you to build strength or power. Heavy resistance training will give you the strength and power you want, but it will not give you much cardiovascular conditioning or endurance.

Neither resistance training nor aerobics will give you the flexibility you need to be graceful. Running will make you "light on your feet," and resistance training will give you power in your body, but neither of these types of exercises is specifically designed to give you flexibility.

No exercise program is worth the trouble unless it gives you all four of the ingredients of physical activity: strength, power, endurance, and flexibility. Let's talk for a moment about what these physical attributes are and how you train for them.

Setting Things Straight

First, let's get our definitions straight so we'll all be talking the same language. Many of the myths about weight training that keep women from trying it spring from misunderstandings about what "resistance" exercise and "weight training" mean. Let's clear up all the myths and mysteries at the very beginning.

Resistance Exercises

"Resistance" training involves contracting muscles against some form of resistance. Weight training is a form of resistance exercise in which the resistance is provided (usually) by iron or cement-filled vinyl plates of varying sizes and weights, which are attached to iron or steel bars. Machines such as Nautilus or Universal feature metal plates stacked on runners and attached to handles or foot pads by chains or cables. But whether you are working out with free weights or with a weighted machine, you are literally lifting weights. In short, you're working against the force of gravity.

Resistance can be provided by other means, in addition to, or instead of, weights. The Unique Athletic Equipment Company uses wide rubber bands. Hydra-Fitness machines use adjustable hydraulic cylinders. Keiser machines use compressed air. Soloflex machines use rubber bungees.

In addition to the type of resistance employed, exercises are also classified according to the range and rapidity of movements. For example, if the resistance against which you are pushing or pulling equals the amount of effort you are exerting, there will be no movement at all. This is called an isometric exercise. Example: push against a brick wall. Your muscles are tensed, but there is no movement of the limbs at the joints, hence no "range of motion."

Another kind of resistance exercise is called isotonic, in which you push or pull against a resistance but your effort is greater than the resistance encountered. In this case, there is a range of motion (your arm will straighten if you're pushing or bend if you're pulling). Barbells and dumbbells provide the most popular form of isotonic exercise.

Isokinetic is the name given to yet another type of resistance exercise in which there is a range of motion and you push or pull against a resistance but the speed at which you make the motion is regulated. This is usually accomplished hydraulically, by devices such as the Cybex machine.

The Hydra-Fitness company has pioneered a fourth type of resistance exercise called *omnikinetic,* in which the amount of resistance can be varied both by adjustment of hydraulic cylinders and by the speed at which the movements are made. The result is a truly simultaneous aerobic and resistance workout.

Further, the terms *strength, power,* and *endurance* have technical meanings. *Strength* is a measure of how much resistance you can overcome, without regard to the amount of time it takes you to do it. *Power,* on the other hand, is a measure of how fast you can overcome a resistance. *Endurance* refers to how many consecutive times you can overcome a resistance. Consequently, you can have strength or power but not much endurance. Or you can have plenty of endurance but no real power.

Weight training is a popular form of resistance exercise used by bodybuilders to make their muscles grow larger; by Olympic weightlifters and powerlifters to give their muscles strength and power; and by everybody from skiers to football players for general muscular conditioning. And since the publication of the original *Bodysculpture,* it has been used by women to lose fat and sculpt their bodies.

Training for shape, on the one hand, or for strength, on the other, is a matter of the way you train. The movements made in the exercises themselves remain the same whether you are a bodybuilder, a weightlifter, or simply someone who wants to fit into last year's bikini without hanging out over the drawstring.

Whether they are done with weights or with hydraulic cylinder machines, resistance exercises are perfect for women's bodyshaping because they can be used to tone up and, with special workout programs, actually sculpt and enhance the natural contours of the body when the problem is sagging or undeveloped musculature. In addition, resistance training provides a way in which circulation can be dramatically increased to and through specific segments of the body. This action helps to overcome common water-retention problems that seem to inhibit fat burning and to initiate a whole spectrum of toning, trimming, and muscle strengthening effects.

Aerobic Exercises

"Aerobics" and "cardiovascular fitness" are among the most popular fitness buzzwords. Much money has been made in the women's health club business by building ad campaigns around such programs as "aerobic dancing," and "aerobic floor exercises." The popular cable TV show "Aerobicize" featuring the gorgeous Nina Rocca, has developed a cult following among both women and men.

Amid all the buzzwords there are some fundamental facts that we need to know about what constitutes "aerobic" exercise and "cardiovascular fitness." Let's begin with "fitness." There are many kinds of fitness:

fitness of a muscle to contract against a resistance, fitness of the joints to bend without injury or strain, and fitness of the nervous system to respond to loads and stresses. But cardiovascular fitness is measured in terms of the capacity of the heart to do work.

The cardiovascular system consists of the heart, the arteries that carry oxygenated blood into the system, and the veins that bring deoxygenated blood back to the heart. Cardiovascular fitness has to do with the ability of the system to work efficiently in carrying and utilizing oxygen. Aerobic exercises condition the cardiovascular system to be fit. And the greater your cardiovascular fitness, the better able you will be to respond effectively to exercises that require lots of oxygen to perform, i.e., endurance exercises.

But what is it that makes an exercise aerobic? The range of answers varies widely. For example, Dr. Gabe Mirkin (you've heard him on NBC radio with his "Gabe Mirkin on Fitness" programs) says that to achieve cardiovascular fitness you must push the heartbeat to more than 60 percent of its maximum for at least 30 minutes, and you must do this at least three times a week.

On the other hand, Dr. Kenneth Cooper, the person who popularized the term *aerobics* (and who is appalled at some of the programs that are passed off as being aerobic when they really aren't), says that if a person gets his or her pulse rate up to around 150 beats per minute, the effect that produces cardiovascular fitness begins about 5 minutes into the exercise bout and continues for the duration of the bout.

Although doctors differ about the details of heart rate and exercise duration, they agree that to achieve a "training effect" in which your cardiovascular fitness increases with each exercise period, you must push your heart rate to a substantial percentage of your capacity and keep it there for an extended period of time.

The real controversy, it seems, centers on the kinds of exercise various authorities accept as aerobic. Mirkin, citing the President's Council on Physical Fitness and Sports, lists as good aerobic training such activities as jogging and running (tied for first place), bicycling, swimming, skating, skiing, handball, and squash.

Cooper, on the other hand, rates these activities on his now-famous point system and cites (in descending order of effectiveness) running, swimming, cycling, walking, stationary running, and handball/squash/basketball. It should be remembered that these activities work only if you perform them with enough élan to get your heart rate up to the speed required for the training effect.

Dr. Cooper and his wife, interviewed on a recent news broadcast, are stumping for mandatory certification of aerobic exercise instructors. According to the Coopers, most of what is called "aerobic" by the studios simply isn't—which means that there may be a lot of fun and jumping around, but that that alone is not sufficient *sustained* exertion to achieve a training effect.

While most physicians scoff at weight training as an aerobic exercise, Dr. Paul DeVore, a frequent contributor to *Iron Man* magazine (one of the oldest and most respected weight training publications) points out that if you simply reduce the length of or do away with the traditional rest period between lifting sets, you will be able to sustain the pulse rate required for aerobic training.

In fact, a Syracuse University study published in 1980 cites an experiment in which 15 different pieces of Dynamics health equipment (weighted exercise machines that work different parts of the body) were used by 12 female and 10 male students. The subjects were studied during 36 sessions of circuit training (moving from machine to machine without resting between exercises). At the end of a 12-week period, all subjects showed significant increases in cardiovascular respiratory endurance.

Further, in a soon-to-be-published study, Dr. Frank Katch has noted no significant difference in cardiovascular fitness between subjects who trained for only six months on Hydra-Fitness omnikinetic machines and other subjects who spent the same period doing nothing but running.

The most effective combination of resistance and endurance exercises seems to be found in a program that combines the two into a single routine such as a circuit through several machines. These special routines are called super-circuits, and they involve interspersing clearly aerobic exercises between traditional resistance exercises. Hence you might follow a bench press bout with three laps around the track followed in turn by a set of arm curls, which are followed by a three-minute set of jumping jacks.

Why all the interest in aerobic exercises? Because they burn calories, that's why. Which brings us to the reasons people work out in the first place. Women seem to want more than anything to lose fat. Secondarily, they want to be able to do their chosen recreational sports with vigor and agility. Men seem to want either strength and health or speed and endurance.

So aerobic exercises have proved popular among women because they burn off the fat. But merely losing fat is not enough to sculpt the body. By now we've all seen the running nuts: people who started jogging to lose a few pounds, then became addicted to running and have now catabolized both the fat and the meat from every part of their bodies but their legs. Their faces are drawn and wan, their skin is leathery from daily runs through the park in subfreezing temperatures. They lost the fat, but they lost most of everything else, too.

Running and jogging work the upper body and the arms only indirectly. The primary work is done by the legs. Consequently, if you want to firm up your bust, you would be better off doing bench presses than you would doing 5-mile runs.

Aerobic Resistance Exercises: The *Bodysculpture Plus* Program

The obvious answer to the question of how to develop a total body exercise and bodyshaping program is to combine aerobic, resistance, and flexibility exercises in order to take advantage of the unique benefits of each type of activity. No matter what Dr. Cooper might think, we think it's just as scandalous that runners have no explosive power in their arms as it is that powerlifters aren't able to run a mile without falling over in a dead faint. It's equally silly to be strong and have endurance but to be so stiff that you have all the grace of a toy robot.

Besides, by combining resistance and aerobic exercise in the same program, you can sculpt body contours, lose body fat, build undeveloped areas, and achieve both muscular and cardiovascular fitness. And the *Bodysculpture Plus* program makes another contribution: it gives you training for agility, flexibility, and gracefulness at the same time that it gives you muscular and cardiovascular fitness.

The last point is an important one. If your exercise program consists *only* of lifting weights, you will find that you'll begin to feel clunky: unable to move around in a hurry or with any agility. If your exercise program consists *only* of jogging or long, slow runs, you will find that you can endure forever but without any real spirit of joy about what you are doing. We repeat: the best program is one that combines resistance, aerobic, flexibility, and agility exercises.

The *Bodysculpture Plus* program gives you strength and power with its resistance exercises, cardiovascular fitness with its aerobic exercises, flexibility with its karate and Yoga stretching exercises, and agility with its dance routines. *Combined in a total-body program that also includes getting your body and soul together,* Bodysculpture Plus *provides the only exercise program that trains your psyche as well as your body for maximum progress and long-term as well as short-term results.*

AEROBIC EXERCISES

Let's follow the experts in adding an aerobic component to our resistance program. Let's list the types of aerobic activities that you will be performing along with other exercises:

1. *Running:* If you work out in a health club, you can do a couple of turns around the track before, after, or between resistance sets.
2. *Stationary cycling:* Many clubs also have stationary bicycles, which will give you an aerobic workout and also will not be hard on your ankle, knee, and hip joints.
3. *Running in place:* Although it is not as efficient as jogging, running, or cycling, running in place will suffice if you are working out at home or do not have access to a running track or a stationary bike.
4. *Jumping jacks:* Still less efficient but easy to do when your workout space is limited.
5. *Swimming:* A good aerobic exercise if you really go at it and don't just loll around the pool.

We've deliberately omitted aerobic dancing routines from the *Bodysculpture Plus* program. Dancing is a top-notch agility developer, but it has limited efficiency as an aerobic activity. The popularity of aerobic

Running in place:
Nina Nicolai and Staara

Jumping jacks:
Nina Nicolai and Staara

dancing programs usually results more from the fun and socialization of dancing in a group than from its aerobic effectiveness.

In this chapter we've designed several types of programs, each of which fills a specific need (such as general conditioning or specific body-part routines). We've also designed a modular format that will enable you to work out your own program that is perfectly fitted to your own personal needs. The Total-Body Conditioning Program is a general conditioner and also the foundation for everything from a general fat-loss program to a full-blown women's bodybuilding program.

Remember that the important thing in aerobic activities is to reach and sustain your target pulse rate. You won't get any training effect if you reach the target pulse rate and sustain it for only three minutes. Conversely, you will derive little aerobic value from exercises that never push your heart rate up to its proper level.

One final *caveat* about any strenuous program (and combining aerobic and resistance routines *is* strenuous!): SEE YOUR DOCTOR FIRST!!!! We can't overstress this point. Knowing what exercises accomplish which physical goals is one thing, but knowing whether or not you personally should be doing those exercises is quite another. *See your doctor. Show him or her the routines in this book. Ask for an opinion about your physical condition and the advisability of following these routines.* If you're in good health, the programs listed in this chapter will do the job for you. But if you are not in good health, you shouldn't even think about doing them without placing yourself under a doctor's supervision.

And please don't think that we're being negative about all this. The point of exercise is to be fit. If you can shape your body and look the way you want to look while at the same time increasing strength, power, endurance, flexibility, and agility, then you've realized a marvelous bonus: you've improved your looks and your health at the same time. *But no look is worth endangering your health.* Develop the body type you have to its fullest potential. You'll look terrific and you'll feel terrific, too. But don't take unnecessary risks just to fit into a certain size dress. You owe yourself more consideration than that.

Women's Bodybuilding Programs

While we're on the subject of good health, now is as good a time as any to talk about women's bodybuilding. The reactions of both men and women to women bodybuilders range from "Wow, look at that!" all the way to "Yuk! How could she do that to herself?"

Women's bodybuilding, like men's bodybuilding, is, at its best, an aesthetic approach to the potential of the human body. For the bodybuilder nothing is more beautiful than fully developed, symmetrical muscular contours. The men work for a balance between massiveness and muscular separation. Women work for a slender, graceful, but chiseled, muscular look. Are the women trying to be men? Nope. Not a chance. Wrong hormones, wrong genes. Can't do it. Women just don't grow big muscles.

"But," you say, "how about the woman I saw on the 'Freak for a Day' show? They sure looked like men to me." Well, relax. There are several things that you must understand about women's bodybuilding in order to appreciate both the achievement and the work that goes into it. Here are the most important things to remember:

1. Many of the supermuscular competitive women bodybuilders you see in the muscle magazines did not get that way by working out with weights. One of the scandals in women's bodybuilding is the fact that many of the top women in the field (especially in the beginning) are *not* weight trainers but gymnasts, dancers, skaters, or swimmers who stepped up their body-conditioning routines and combined them with a superstrict diet.

2. Women have a terrible time developing any muscle size at all. To overcome the problem of being born with the wrong hormones for muscular hypertrophy, many (in fact, most) of the competitive women bodybuilders take anabolic steroids to enhance muscle growth and fat loss.

3. Since even with steroids women have great difficulty achieving gains in muscle size, the criteria for judging women's competition have evolved toward extreme muscularity—which means a body-fat percentage down around 3 or 4 percent.

4. When a woman's body-fat percentage gets that low, she stops menstruating. The same thing happens to runners. It's nothing new. But it is cause for reflection about side effects, such as impaired fertility and loss of secondary sex characteristics.

5. Stringent diets are part of the women's bodybuilding game. And so are mineral supplements, protein supplements, and loads of vitamins. It can be expensive.

6. We are personally acquainted with numerous competitive women bodybuilders. Many of them leave competition after a couple of years because they don't see the logic in risking their health for a few titles and some brass trophies.

7. If you are really planning to be a competitive woman bodybuilder,

you must plan on working out two hours a day, five days a week, to beat your body into the shape expected for competition.

8. If you want to be a competitive woman bodybuilder you must develop an athlete's self-discipline, because that's what these women are: athletes.

Sounds like a lot, doesn't it? Well, it is. *If you don't want to look the way women bodybuilders look, don't worry. There is absolutely no way in the world that you are ever going to accidentally work out too hard and by mistake get to look the way they do.* No way in the world. It takes incredible commitment, blitzing and bombing workouts, pushing yourself way beyond what you ever thought you could do, and keeping at it every day, day after day. Smart women are training for health as well as looks.

Who would want to be a woman bodybuilder? Literally thousands of women all across America. They're a new breed of superwoman, and they're changing the ways that both women and men think about women. If you want to join them, the exercises in this book are the ones they use. Just push yourself to the limit as any competitive athlete would and give it everything you've got. That's the difference between bodybuilding and bodyshaping. It's the difference between athletics and bodysculpture. It's all a matter of the amount of effort you want to expend. If you want to be a real woman bodybuilder, look forward to four and five days a week of one- to three-hour workouts.

But if you simply want to look good, slim down, be fit and strong—spending only three or four hours a week working out—then the *Bodysculpture Plus* program will give you everything you need for fast, effective progress.

Bodysculpture Plus Programs

Now that we know all the exercises and all the ins and outs of putting them together to form a total-body program, let's turn to the routines themselves. We'll list them in the order of difficulty, starting with the least difficult and building up to advanced training routines. Remember that you should always begin any workout with a warm-up. If you have trouble psyching up for a workout, follow the ritual suggested in Chapter 3.

WARM-UP AND/OR FLEXIBILITY EXERCISES

1. *The Yoga stretching routine in Chapter 4*
2. *The ballet routine in Chapter 4*
3. *The modern dance routine in Chapter 4*
4. *The karate stretching routine in Chapter 4*
   (*Note:* Do all the exercises with fluidity of movement).

AGILITY EXERCISES

Do any of the four exercise routines listed above. Start the exercise movements in slow motion, gradually increasing the speed of your movements. Then, as your speed increases, flow from one movement directly into the next so that you do them without rest between the movements. These are exercises for agility; strive for fluidity and grace, timing and balance. These exercises can be combined with resistance and aerobic routines as semi-rest periods.

Routine 1: Beginning Resistance Conditioning

Exercises	page
Warm-up (Yoga routine)	63–74
Squat	86
Bench press	115
Calf raise	93
Arm curl	127
Crunch with feet on a bench	100
Leg curl	90
Regular deadweight lift	106
Shrug	111
Spinal hyperextension on the floor	104
Cool-down (walk with decreasing speed for 1 minute)	

The purpose of the beginning resistance conditioning routine: If you are a beginner or have not exercised for some time, the general conditioning routine will bring your strength and endurance up to a level sufficient to allow you to go on to more advanced routines. It is a total-body workout. It works the muscles in groups. Don't worry about specializing in specific body parts yet. First you have to develop general muscular fitness and endurance.

Number of repetitions and amount of weight to use: At the beginning you should use enough weight to enable you to do only 8 repetitions (reps) of the particular exercise movement. Work out every other day. Add one repetition to each exercise movement (if possible) every fourth workout day.

When to add weight: When you reach 16 repetitions in all the exercises, drop back to 8 reps and add weight. You should be able to add 2½ to 5 pounds to the arm movements and 5 to 10 pounds to the leg and back movements. Concentrate on each movement. Try not to let anything interfere with your concentration.

Routine 2: Advanced Resistance Conditioning

Exercises	*page*
Warm-up (karate routine plus 3 minutes of running)	48–62
Squat	86
Bench press	115
Calf raise	93
Arm curl	127
Crunch with the feet on a bench	100
Seated press	123
Leg curl	90
Regular deadweight lift	106
Seated twist	52

Routine 2 *(cont.)*

Exercise	page
Spinal hyperextension on a Roman bench	105
Shrug	111
Vertical or forward leg raise	105
Cool-down (walk with decreasing speed for 3 minutes, then do 30 crunches on the floor)	

Purpose of the advanced general conditioning resistance routine: This routine is a step on the way to the aerobic/resistance routine. You should supplement this routine by running or jogging on your off days. In addition to the beginning resistance exercises, we've added the seated press for concentration on the triceps muscles of the upper arm and a vertical or forward raise for the lower abdominal muscles. We've also moved you up in the crunch and the hyperextension to a Roman bench. Thirty additional crunches are added at the end as part of the cool-down.

Number of repetitions and amount of weight to use: Follow the guidelines specified in the beginning routine.

When to add weight: Follow the guidelines specified in the beginning routine.

Routine 3: Beginning Aerobic/Resistance Conditioning

Exercises	page
Warm-up (Yoga or karate routine)	48–74
Squat	86
Jumping jacks (10 seconds)	
Rest (10 seconds)	
Bench press	115

Routine 3 *(cont.)*

Exercises	page
Jumping jacks (10 seconds)	
Rest (10 seconds)	
Arm curl	127
Calf raise	93
Running in place (10 seconds)	
Crunch with feet on a bench	100
Leg curl	90
Jumping jacks (10 seconds)	
Rest (10 seconds)	
Regular deadweight lift	106
Spinal hyperextension on the floor or on a Roman bench	105
Running in place (10 seconds)	
Shrug	111
Cool-down (walk with decreasing speed for 1 minute)	

Purpose of the beginning aerobic/resistance conditioning routine: The purpose of this routine is to build strength while building endurance. Few people combine these two different types of exercises. It will take you a short time to get used to the extra stress.

Pace at which the routine should be done: Timing and pacing are everything in an aerobic resistance routine. The point is to reach your target pulse rate and to sustain it for longer than 15 minutes. Don't use so much weight in the resistance exercises that you are unable to perform the aerobic component. Conversely, don't perform the aerobic exercises so vigorously that you have no strength to do the resistance exercises. Start slowly and work up to it. You don't have to reach your target pulse rate the first time you do the routine. If it really knocks you out, go back to the beginning general conditioning routine and supplement it with a run around the track or running in place after the resistance workout.

Number of repetitions and amount of weight to use: Follow the guidelines specified in the beginning resistance routine, adding the caveat about pacing cited above.

When to add weight: Follow the guidelines specified in the beginning routine.

Routine 4: Advanced Aerobic/Resistance Conditioning

Exercises	*page*
Warm-up (karate stretches; no rest between movements)	48–62
Running or cycling (1 minute at a moderate pace)	
Squat	86
Jumping jacks (30 seconds)	
Crunch with feet on a bench	100
Calf raise	93
Running or cycling (30 seconds at a moderate rate)	
Walking rest (15 seconds—vary with pulse rate)	
Arm curl	127
Seated twist	52
Seated press	123
Jumping jacks (30 seconds)	
Leg curl	90
Spinal hyperextension on a Roman bench	105
Regular deadweight lift	106
Fast walking or running in place (30 seconds)	
Shrug	111

Routine 4 (*cont.*)

Exercises	page
Vertical or forward leg raise	105
Running or cycling (20 seconds)	
Reclining lateral leg raise	57
Running or cycling (5 minutes)	
Cool-down (walking at decreasing speed; then 30 crunches)	

Purpose of the advanced aerobic/resistance routine: One of the prerequisites of any physical activity is to be able to sustain one's effort long enough to see real progress. When it comes to general total-body conditioning routines, the Advanced Aerobic/Resistance routine is one of the most difficult around. If you are already in top shape, however, you can add to the routine's difficulty simply by extending the duration of the aerobic component.

Number of repetitions and amount of weight: Follow the guidelines specified in the beginning routine.

When to add weight: Follow the guidelines specified in the beginning routine.

General Comments on the General Conditioning Routines
No matter what your bodyshaping/fitness goals are, you should begin your *Bodysculpture Plus* program with one of these four routines. If you are completely out of shape, just do the Yoga and/or karate stretches for a week, and then start Routine Number One. If you're already in fairly good shape, go right into Routine Number Two. If you are in better than average shape, start with Routine Number Three. If you are really in top shape, try starting with Routine Number Four.
No matter where you start, you should do a general conditioning routine for 30 days before you move on to the specific body area routines. This will prevent injury and make your progress in bodyshaping faster and more effective. When you begin the specific area

routines, you shouldn't abandon the general conditioning routines. Instead, you should alternate between general conditioning and specific area routines from one workout day to the next (for example, do general conditioning on Monday, a specific area routine on Wednesday, and general conditioning on Friday).

You should always include a general conditioning routine in your workout program even if your goals are directed to only one part of your body (such as whittling down your waist). Each of these routines will work the entire body. Numbers One and Two concentrate on strength and power. Numbers Three and Four combine strength and power conditioning with cardiovascular conditioning.

In summary:

1. The aerobic component of the routines will speed up body-fat loss and aid in cardiovascular conditioning.
2. The resistance exercises will give you strength (if you do the movements slowly), power (if you do the movements quickly), and muscular endurance (if you start with 12 reps and work up to 20 reps in the lifts instead of using the 8–16 reps format).
3. The inclusion of Yoga, karate, dance routines in the warm-up periods and cool-downs provides you with general flexibility and agility training.
4. The psyching-up advice in Chapter 3 will help you to succeed in reaching your goals and in keeping the gains you've made.

Result: a total-body routine that gives you everything you need to look terrific, feel terrific, and be terrific!

BODYSCULPTURE PLUS ROUTINES FOR SPECIFIC AREA BODYSHAPING

You've worked your way through Routine Number Three and you're anxious to start working on specific problems areas. Stick it out for 30 days. The only exception would be if you are able to start with Routine Number Four. If you're in that kind of shape, start alternating specific area routines with the general conditioning routine.

The specific area routines listed below are the ones for which we've had the greatest number of requests over the past five years. Here are the general rules for doing them:

1. **Number of Repetitions:** start with 10 reps and go to 20 before dropping back to 10 reps and adding weight.
2. **Amount of Weight:** use as much weight as you can handle for the prescribed number of repetitions.
3. **Form:** do all of the exercises in strict form. Don't cheat by tossing the weights up. Make the individual muscles do the work by themselves.
4. Do 3 sets of each exercise (a "set" consists of a single series of repetitions of a specific exercise movement. For example, "2 sets of 10 reps in the arm curl" means that you would do 10 repetitions of the arm curl, rest for 30 seconds, then do 10 more repetitions).
5. Don't rest longer than 30 seconds between sets.

Got it? Here are the specific area routines:

Specific Area Routine 1: Hips and Thighs

Exercises	*page*
Warm-up (3 minutes running or 3 minutes cycling)	
Squat	86
Jumping jacks (45 seconds)	
Leg extension	89
Running in place (get the knees as high as you can)	
Crunch (as an "active rest" exercise)	100
Leg curl	90
Jumping jacks (45 seconds)	
Reclining lateral leg raise	57
Standing posterior leg raise	94
X-Rated hip exercise	96
Running or cycling (work up to 20 minutes)	

Specific Area Routine 2: Waist

Exercises	page
Warm-up (5 minutes of running or cycling)	
Vertical leg raise	105
Running in place (get the knees as high as you can)	
Spinal hyperextension on the floor	104
Running or cycling (1 minute)	
Crunch (start with the easiest one and work up to the crunch in a lotus position)	100
Jumping jacks (1 minute)	
Side leans	103
Bentover twist (2 minutes)	103
Running or cycling (5 minutes)	
Seated twists (5 minutes)	52

Specific Area Routine 3: Arms and Chest

Exercises	page
Warm-up (running or cycling for 5 minutes)	
Karate arm movements	53
Bench press	115
Jumping jacks (2 minutes)	
Arm curl	127
Seated press	123
Running or cycling (1 minute)	

Arms and Chest *(cont.)*

Exercises	page
Crunch (as an "active rest" exercise)	100
Flyes	117
Jumping jacks (1 minute)	
Bent-arm pullover	120
Concentrated curl	128
Triceps extension	131
Running or cycling (10 minutes)	

HOW TO DEVELOP YOUR OWN PERSONALIZED *BODYSCULPTURE PLUS* PROGRAM

You now have all the information about exercises and programs you'll ever need to do all the bodyshaping you could ever want to do. And if you have problem areas other than the ones for which the 3 specific area programs were designed, all you have to do is look up the exercises that work those problem areas and plug them into your own personalized specific area program.

That's why we indexed the exercises under body areas (starting on page 196). Just remember to alternate your specific area program with the general conditioning routines as described above. There's no way that you won't succeed. All you've got to do is follow the routines in the program.

The Next Step

Now, the next step: what's the single most important element in a successful weight-loss, bodyshaping routine *besides* initiative, determination, and the *Bodysculpture Plus* aerobic/resistance exercise programs? DIET!

Yes, *diet.* You've got to eat meals that are balanced between carbohydrates, proteins, and fats. You've got to find that fine line between eating too much to lose any fat and eating too little to sustain you in your *Bodysculpture Plus* program. And that's the next step that Valerie will show you in Chapter 7.

Chapter 7

What to Do
About Your Diet

"What, me diet?" you may have said a hundred times to your well-meaning friends. You're *always* on a diet. One week it's Dr. Atkins, another week, it's only diet powder and liquid protein. One month you yo-yo down 10 pounds and fit into your new jeans; the next month you yo-yo up and hide in your tent dresses again. Your wardrobe bulges with size 16s for the fat times and 8s for the lean ones.

And then there's your cousin, the diet junkie, who has tried every pill, liquid supplement, meal-in-a-can, powder, and capsule in the book. She's into fish only this week, vitamin pills and passion fruit the next. She's reed thin, of course—but she's also nervous, jittery, tired, and hyperactive. And she complains of thinning hair and cold hands and feet all the time.

So what's the real story on diet? Why can't we, with all our sophisticated knowledge about diet and nutrition, and our current level of diet know-how, control our weight and keep it down? As we noted in the "Fat Demon" chapter, over 90 percent of people who lose 20 pounds or more regain it within six months, sometimes with interest.

The problem all goes back to a real schizophrenia in our culture. Pick up a magazine—any magazine—from the newsstand or from your coffee table at home, and you'll see what we mean.

The latest feature will probably be an excerpt from Miss Celebrity Star's latest book, *Celebrity Star's Beauty, Diet, and Exercise Guide*, replete with photos of Celebrity herself weighing not an ounce over 105 pounds. Read on in the magazine and there will be diet success stories, diet tips, diets for working mothers, diets for pregnant women, diets for teenagers, and diets for grandmothers. There will be ads for diet plans, calorie-controlled foods, magic weight-loss pills and formulas.

But dip into the other ads and features, and it's another story. There's a whole world of mouth-watering pictures and recipes for double fudge sundaes, steaming casseroles of lasagna, calorie-dense creams and sauces, steaming soups and stews, and just to top it off, a hot buttered rum for a windy afternoon. You can guess where the poor reader's New Year's resolutions just went!

It's a simple fact of life: eating is one of our chief pleasures. It's the basis of so many of our social/romantic/business occasions: the business lunch; happy hour with munchies; the leisurely Sunday brunch; the intimate dinner *à deux;* the five-course, five-star banquet; the hearty country holiday feast. Food is the way we celebrate our successes, toast business and romantic liaisons, make deals, console ourselves and our friends. Food figures in our marriages, christenings, graduations, confirmations, bar/bas mitzvahs, birthdays, retirements, even funerals. It's a source of comfort, pleasure, nostalgia, romance and, yes, aesthetic satisfaction.

Contrast what happens when we "go on a diet." We are cast out, however temporarily, from the world of patés and pizza, chocolate and cheese, and consigned to a dreary regimen of lettuce leaves, plain yogurt, grapefruit sections, and water-packed tuna. Faced with that, no wonder we backslide into the sins of the palate so easily!

Fortunately, the new diet-consciousness of the late seventies and the eighties does carry some benefits for us all—and one is the sudden spate of foods that are both good and good for us. We've gone a long way, all of us, since the days of meals-in-a-can. Now a dieter can choose between frozen gourmet dinners, nouvelle cuisine, or, if he/she prefers Italian cookery, low-sodium, low-cal pasta entrées. There's even low-cal Tex-Mex and diet pizza, not to mention diet sodas that taste like the real thing and are both sodium-free and caffeine-free. Shops in major cities cater to the dieter's sweet tooth and make wondrous flourless and sugarless low-cal chocolate goodies.

So you're in luck! No matter how hard you may have found dieting before, now is your time. The perpetual dieter has come into her own. So read on and learn how to fight the Fat Demon and still enjoy your favorite foods!

Get Ready for Your Diet

If "psyching up" is part of exercise, it's also a big part of getting started on any diet. If you're like most of us, you've got a refrigerator and pantry full of forbidden goodies. Start by cleaning up. Donate the high-calorie snacks or mixes to your church or favorite charity. Or share them with a skinny friend. Just get them out of the house; otherwise you'll find yourself, some fine night when the moon is full, boiling up a plate of pasta topped with marshmallow whip and peanut butter. Diets have been known to produce strange cravings.

When your shelves and refrigerator are bare, or nearly so, go out shopping for the right stuff—the things you'll need for your new diet. How much of any one item you'll need to buy depends very much on your individual habits and life-style. But try to have these things on hand, at least:

- Plenty of mineral water (Perrier or Ramlosa if you like carbonated water, Evian if you like it uncarbonated)
- Caffeine-free, sodium-free diet sodas
- Unsweetened juices, vegetable and fruit
- Herbs and spices for seasoning
- Vanilla flavoring
- Cinnamon sticks and whole cloves for coffee and tea
- Salt and sugar substitutes
- Fresh lemons
- Plain low-fat yogurt or an artificially flavored fruit yogurt (no sugar)
- Low-fat cottage cheese
- Diet syrup or imitation honey/molasses
- Coffees and teas (the more exotic the better)
- Low-sodium soups and soup mixes
- Vegetable oil for cooking; also a nonstick pan coating such as Pam
- Melba toast, bran wafers, or flatbread
- Plain wheat germ or bran flakes
- Unsalted seeds, soy nuts, and raisins for snacks
- Raw fruits and vegetables
- Water-packed tuna (or salmon) and chicken (both low-sodium)
- Eggs
- Low-fat cheeses

These will be the "staples" of your diet. You will want to put together some special meals, of course (see the weekend portion of our Start-Up Diet for ideas), but these staples will assure that you do not come home some evening to an empty refrigerator and the overwhelming temptation to send out for a pizza. If you're in a hurry in the morning, you can always have a quick breakfast of juice and low-fat yogurt. Low-fat cheese and fresh fruit make a delicious, quick snack. More often than not, it's the "there's nothing to eat in the house" trap that sends us scurrying to the nearest Wendy's in search of not only the beef but the bun, the ketchup, the mustard, the mayonnaise . . .

If your family isn't joining you on this diet, at least officially, try to keep their foods out of your way as much as possible. And try, unofficially, to introduce them to some small but significant changes: diet drinks instead of regular colas, low-fat cheeses and butter instead of the regular, fat-laden variety, more fish and chicken and less beef and pork. If you make the changes subtle and appetizing enough, they might just discover that they prefer your way of eating to theirs.

Make Your Diet Meals Fun

When we talked about the aesthetics of dieting a few pages ago, we weren't just blowing smoke. Psychologists tell us that about 50 percent to 60 percent of any meal is "eaten" with the eyes and nose. In other words, the actual taste of the food we consume is often less important than how it looks and smells, even how it feels in our hands and on the tongue. That's why we often overeat in a restaurant or at a party while we can stick religiously to a diet when we eat in the office lunchroom or at home. The restaurant and party food is so attractive, so interesting-looking, that we lose control and eat more than we want or need.

But we can learn from those restaurant or party presentations to make diet meals seem interesting and important. Instead of gulping down cottage cheese and yogurt straight from the carton, serve it up in style. Here's how: Start by bringing out the most attractive table linens you have. Set the table with big, attractive place mats in straw, linen, or cotton—vinyl or Plexiglas if you're going high-tech. Use Grandma's finest lace, cutwork tea napkins, table runners, or hunt up some replicas in your local antique shop. Have elegant linen napkins, or big colorful oversized paper ones, candles, fresh flowers, a side dish of fresh vegetables or fruit. Put on your favorite record or tape cassette for mood music. Arrange everything on attractive plates (a little smaller than dinner-sized so you'll feel you're eating a lot).

Expand the eye appeal by garnishing everything you serve with parsley, watercress, lemon or lime wedges, or thin slices of fruit. Whole kumquats or lady apples and small wedges of kiwi or passion fruit will help fill up the plates and add color. So will small clusters of grapes, fresh cranberries, or sections of tangerines or Mandarin oranges. Sliced green peppers, onion rings, a wedge of red cabbage, or julienne carrots add spark to a vegetarian meal.

For drinkables, splurge on a bottle of the best mineral water you can find. Serve it in chilled frosted goblets straight out of the freezer—and don't forget the wedge of lime or lemon.

For hors d'oeuvres, make a tray of fresh crudites (raw veggies) by cutting up cauliflower, broccoli, carrots, zucchini, cucumbers, cherry tomatoes, mushrooms, and green or red peppers. Serve with a centerpiece bowl of yogurt-dill dip. A tasty and filling starter for your diet meals! Or make a production out of a huge dinner salad with low-calorie dressing—almost a meal in itself!

For dessert, layer a diet parfait of dietetic gelatin and fresh fruit in tall chilled glasses. Or simply serve a very continental-looking plate of fruit with a few wedges of low-fat cheese; there are now some delicious, subtle ones on the market that don't have the papery taste of those a few years ago. Follow it with a cup of steaming espresso with a twist of lemon rind or coffee with cinnamon sticks and a tiny dollop of mock whipped cream. You'll get up from the table feeling refreshed, not deprived, and ready to stay on your diet. You've simply replaced quantity with quality and further motivated yourself to stay on the program.

Avoid the Cheap/Fast–Foods Traps

We dieters have a number of ways to psych ourselves out of as well as into diets. And one of the most common ways is with the cheap/fast–food trap.

The trap goes like this: "I don't have the money to diet. I'm on a strict budget and dieting is expensive. All that steak and fresh fish and fresh produce and all the special foods. Who has that kind of money?" Or this: "I don't have time to diet. I work late nearly every night, and then I often go on to a meeting or out to dinner with friends. I eat nearly every meal away from home, and you just can't diet in restaurants. And all those business lunches . . . and I never have the time to make myself a decent meal . . ."

Excuses, excuses! Let's take up these objections in order—money first. It's true that some foods we think of as dietetic are expensive. In fact, back in the seventies, a diet they called the Rockefeller Diet was making the rounds: filet mignon three times a day, washed down with the finest wine and nothing else—except the fresh oysters that were out of season and the Iranian caviar and fresh strawberries and raspberries you simply *had* to eat for breakfast. The point was, you had to be a Rockefeller to afford it!

Fortunately, we've grown in nutritional sophistication since those days. The steak, we would note today, is entirely too high in fat, protein, and cholesterol to qualify for anyone's diet. The caviar is salt-loaded and would cause water retention. The fresh berries are the only part of the diet that would pass muster, and any other fresh fruits would do equally well.

Of course, all food is expensive today. But look at the really costly items: the prepackaged stuff, the junk, prepared, and convenience foods, the marbled steak and pork chops, the fatty cuts of other meats. The more modestly priced items are what you should be eating anyway. We've never forgotten a statement made by the late Gloria Swanson and William Dufty on "AM Chicago" in the late seventies when they were promoting his book *Sugar Blues.* Although the two of them traveled with trunks of specially prepared foods and mineral waters, their monthly food bill was less than that of an average welfare family living in New York City.

So you see, our new nutritional sophistication is paying off. We no longer think of steaks as diet food. We're more apt to find diet entrées listed as pasta primavera or herbed chicken or a plain grilled fish. Certainly that's what our own Start-Up Diet features. The items you'll be giving up are both diet no-nos and costly: fat-marbled cuts of meat, expensive breaded, sauced, and creamed entrées, rich desserts, processed cereals, breads, and snack foods. We'll save you money on those items and give you more to put into the real diet foods: low-fat dairy produce, lean meats, fish and fowl, fresh fruits and vegetables, and whole-grain cereals and breads.

Now for the time problem. It seems that everyone these days is on the fast track. We're like the people Bob Greene described in a recent column in the *Chicago Tribune:* we haven't a moment to spare. We cross the country in a day, work while we travel, eat while we work, talk business while we socialize, make calls from our car, shop from our desks. We are all overcommitted, rushed, tense, and often, literally, have no time to eat.

But that's exactly the situation the dieter should prepare for. Because she already has a diet plan thought out in advance, meals cease to be a problem (notice that we've already taken care of that in our Start-Up Diet, in the Monday through Friday meals). Breakfast can be a protein shake or a carton of low-fat yogurt to eat on the way to work. Lunch can be a big tossed salad and fruit downed at your desk or a plain tuna salad (hold the mayo) from the office deli or cafeteria.

Dinner is a frozen diet entrée and salad or fruit nibbled while you catch the evening news and check the figures for your evening meeting or dress for that theater benefit. You can get through the evening without having strayed from your diet and still eat nutritiously. A before-bed snack of whole-grain crackers, or bran wafers and some low-fat cheese with a glass of juice, and you're ready for sweet dreams.

Remember that the superfancy diet cookbooks have done us both a great service and also a disservice. They've given us tremendous variety and innovation in diet menus—and they've also made us feel terribly guilty if we have no time to rustle up a superb dietetic meal every evening. We end up eating our usual carton of cottage cheese and feeling as if we've failed our families and ourselves. It's all part of that Superwoman mythology that every eighties career woman has to shake. Valerie's compromise: we eat on the run Monday through Thursday, then save weekends for the experiments in nouvelle cuisine. That way, we can have an occasional fancy meal and also save time during the week, when we don't have a moment to spare.

A Guide to Current Diets

Each year they come out in droves, usually in the spring: those gorgeous, oh-so-slick diet books. There's *Dr. Soso's Quick Weight Loss Plan, Celebrity Star's Personal 10-Day Diet, The Grosse Pointe Pig-Out Diet Plan,* the *I Love North Dakota Diet Book,* and a host of other weird and wonderful plans. Most of them are based on some gimmick (one bunch of grapes, one tablespoon of cornstarch, six vitamin pills . . .), a single food (eat only veal chops three times a day), some magic formula in liquid or powdered form, or another weight-loss gimmick, all guaranteeing that you'll lose 10 pounds in 10 days if only you follow *this* regimen.

The trouble is, they all work to a limited extent. For anyone who is appreciably overweight—20 pounds or more—cutting back on food intake to any extent for even a week or 10 days will produce some results. And if the diet is restricted enough, even if it's 800 calories per day of chocolate ice cream, you'll lose weight—maybe not a substantial loss, but enough to convince you that this at last is the real thing.

But there's something insidious about all those magical weight-loss formulas. Most of them are woefully unbalanced and as a result, they can be dangerous to your health. Some don't even furnish the minimum requirements necessary to maintain good health. As a result, you'll find yourself lagging in energy, feeling tired, listless, perhaps developing cardiovascular or digestive disturbances from some of the regimens.

So let's look at a few categories of these "new and magical" diets— which may or may not be quite as magical as they sound at first:

ZERO-CALORIE/MINICALORIE PLANS

These programs are either total fasts, liquids-only fasts, or under-500-calories-a-day plans. On the plus side: rapid weight loss (good for the psyche and scales); little or no water retention; and an energetic, "high" feeling. The minuses? Overly fast weight loss, loss of potassium, salt, minerals, and fluids, a disturbed electrolyte balance, and muscle tissue loss instead of real fat loss. A 24-hour fast is usually okay if you have your doctor's consent; longer than that requires serious medical supervision. Better to try a liquids-only program like the Golden Door's liquid day to assure an adequate balance of fluids and minerals if you do decide to try fasting.

SINGLE-FOOD DIETS

These seem to come and go in and out of vogue every year or so. As the name implies, they're diets based on a single food or type of food. Perhaps the most famous of the breed was the infamous Beverly Hills Diet, built basically on 10 days of raw fruit and little else. Celebrities and common folk alike raved about the amount of weight they lost on the diet, but in reality it was mostly massive water loss from the diarrhea the fruit regimen induced. Sure, it gave the dieter plenty of vitamin C and fiber, but the trade-off was too much. Physicians warned Beverly Hills dieters, throughout the summer of 1981, of potassium depletion, electrolyte imbalance leading to cardiac arrhythmia, digestive trouble, irritation of the intestines and colon, and so on. A bit too much just to be able to fit into your Rodeo Drive threads!

Single-food diets usually produce quick, dramatic results because they are based on water loss rather than on real body-fat loss. But most provide insufficient amounts of other nutrients and therefore shortchange basic nutrition in favor of temporary loss. And since they're not diets we can live with for any period of time, they usually don't permanently affect one's eating habits or reeducate one's eating patterns. Result: a month or two hence, you're back where you started from and then some. And you're shopping for a new quick weight-loss diet to enable you to lose the same 10 pounds all over again!

PROTEIN-ONLY DIETS

Let's make some distinctions right at the beginning: limited carbohydrates, yes (within limits); zero carb, no. You need some carbohydrates to avoid ketosis, acidosis, potassium loss, fatigue, and an excess of protein and fat (yes, you *can* take in too much protein—the average woman needs about one gram of protein for every two pounds of body weight and anything else is stored as fat). So among the protein-pushing diets, it's yes to levels one and two of the Atkins Super-Energy Diet, the Scarsdale Diet, the Adrien Arpel "Sacred Cow" Diet, and any other regimen that allows you from 30 to 60 grams of carbohydrates a day. Say no in any language to level one of the Atkins Diet (the zero-carb phase), the Stillman Diet, the various water diets, and all the liquid-protein programs that flooded the market in the late seventies.

Why do high-protein diets produce such quick results? It's simple. Carbohydrates bind two to three times their weight in water, so reducing carb intake releases all the "free" water in the system. Proteins don't have this water-binding property; also, they don't stimulate appetite as carbohydrates do, so you may eat less and therefore stick to your diet. (If you need to be on a low-carbohydrate regimen and it's cleared by your doctor, try Dr. Barbara Edelstein's *The Woman Doctor's Diet for Women*. It's safe, simple, ungimmicky, and includes enough carbohydrates to make it safe for long-term use.)

HIGH-CARB, PROTEIN-POOR DIETS

Just as dangerous as their high-protein relatives are the rice diets, the "salads only" programs, the macrobiotic and vegetarian diets, and those numerous other programs that claim if we'd only drop the animal protein, we would be trim, enlightened, and possessed of boundless energy, not to mention good karma. While it's true almost all of us eat too much fat and protein, and that raw fruits and vegetables are generally healthy fare, it's also worth noting that vegetable proteins are incomplete proteins. You need animal protein (eggs and dairy products qualify) to help digest your tofu, bean sprouts, and alfalfa shoots. And all you over-25s take note: Dr. Edelstein is right when she notes that a diet without protein makes you look haggard!

THE DIET PLAN DIETS

These are generally safe, sane, well-balanced diet plans that provide nutritious meals, careful calorie and portion control, and enough variety to assure that you can stay on the regimen for a longer period of time. Such plans, especially coupled with supportive diet groups, are very useful to the sociable dieter who needs the "buddy system," public weigh-ins, contests, celebrations, newsletters, and group meetings. For some loners, it's more togetherness than they can take. Here you have to be the judge of your individual psyche and its workings.

Note, however, that even if you tend to be a closet dieter, now that the frozen Weight Watchers and Stouffer's low-cal gourmet dinners are available in supermarkets—as are yogurts, butters, cheeses, and even desserts—the portion-control problem is licked forever. You don't have to attend even one meeting to use these products! They're perfect solutions for the busy woman—career person or homemaker—who doesn't have time to cook dietetic meals from scratch.

"THINK YOURSELF THIN" DIET PLANS

Most of these are the sheerest nonsense, based as they are on the assumption that obesity is really a psychological and not a physiological problem and that therefore you can eat all of whatever you want as long as you: eat from one bowl/always eat in the same place/think of the "thin you" as you eat/try acupuncture, hypnosis, rolfing, etc., as you diet. The advantage: if your obesity is really due to psychologically induced overeating, then these head tricks may be exactly what you need to get started. The disadvantage: you may be fooled into thinking that calories don't count or that you can eat anything you want from *your* bowl. Your original overeating may have been psychological in origin, but now it's a simple matter of eating less and moving around more that will get you the figure you want.

THE PRITIKIN PROGRAM

This is probably as close to a "good" diet as any that current books offer. It's sane, nutritionally balanced, stresses long-term losses coupled with responsible exercise programs, and has sufficient variety so that you won't go off the diet the week after you begin.

Moreover, it is high in complex carbohydrates. It's also low in refined sugar and stresses fish and poultry rather than beef and other high-fat, high-cholesterol meats. It's heavy on fiber and vitamins, low in fats. You might need to supplement the regimen with a little more protein if you're doing heavy weight training, but 20 or so extra grams of protein per day can do the trick. You can't go wrong with this one unless you have digestive or intestinal troubles, in which case you should check with your doctor first to make sure that the heavy dose of fiber and roughage is okay for your system to handle.

Learn to Recognize a Good Diet when You See One

In general, the simpler, the less gimmicky a diet is, the more balanced and the better it is. Any good, calorie-controlled, balanced diet will get you where you want to be. Try the AMA diets, the "Dietary Goals for the US" program, the Edelstein diet for women (or for teenage girls, if you're under 20), the American Heart Association diet, the Pritikin diet, or the programs prescribed by Weight Watchers, Overeaters Anonymous, etc. And if you want an easy, one-week program just to get you started, try the one printed at the end of this chapter under the title of the Start-Up Diet.

For the first 7 days of your program we recommend a short-term diet. It's designed to give you an initial drop in pounds and to help maintain strength and stamina as you begin your program of workouts. Or maybe you're already on a diet that works for you. (Be sure to check with your doctor before beginning this or any other diet.) Also, check through this list of questions before you undertake that new diet or continue with an old, tried-and-true one:

1. Does the diet have sufficient variety to allow me to stay on it for a period of time—several months or longer if that's what it takes for me to reach my weight-loss goal?
2. Does the diet have a good balance among proteins, carbohydrates, and fats or is it a one-note diet, stressing one kind of food to the exclusion of others? (Remember that a diet, if it's good, should follow the guidelines suggested by the *Mayo clinic diet manual,*

W. B. Saunders and Co., 1980: 60 percent carbohydrates, 20 percent fats, and 20 percent protein.)

3. Is the diet generally low in fat and cholesterol? If not, and the diet is otherwise generally a good one, can you make low-fat substitutions, such as low-fat dairy products for regular ones?

4. Does the diet stress complex carbohydrates (unrefined grains, breads, cereals, vegetables, and fruits) and not refined sugars, desserts, and junk foods? It's all right to have an occasional simple dessert, but fresh fruit or unsweetened gelatin is better.

5. Is the diet low in sodium and preservatives, such as MSG?

6. Does the diet take into account any food allergies you might have? (For example, a person with a diagnosed wheat allergy would do well to get her complex carbohydrates from rice products, fruits and vegetables, not from wheat-containing breads and cereals.)

7. Does the diet provide sufficient vitamins (A, B1, B2, B6, B12, C, D, E, and K)? If it's deficient in any of these, is a multivitamin supplement also recommended?

8. Does the diet provide plenty of the essential minerals: calcium, sodium, potassium, and magnesium?

9. Does the diet provide sufficient calories for you to continue your workouts as well as your daily work, household chores, and social life without being fatigued? Here's where the minicalorie diets of less than 500 calories per day fall short: they can allow for quick weight loss and can even be nutritionally balanced, but they simply don't supply enough calories for you to carry on your daily activities. Don't try to stay on a regimen of under 800 calories a day without close medical supervision.

10. Does the diet stress short-term goals or a long-term eating plan that will allow you to both take off the weight initially and keep it off?

Dining Out Thin: Avoiding the Restaurant Trap

Statistics show it: women in America between the ages of 22 and 40-plus are eating out more than ever before: on an average of three to four times a week or more. Most of us simply don't have time to cook and even if we did, who wants to slave over a hot stove after a long, hard day at the office or on the road? Restaurant eating is becoming a way of life—but, unfortunately, one that brings with it a whole set of new temptations: new and exotic foods, munchie bars, desserts, and the ever-present bread basket. What's the poor dieter to do?

Fortunately, you don't have to give up on your diet even though you're eating out several times a week. Copy and save (or memorize) this handy list of permissible restaurant foods and you'll find that you don't blow your diet every time you eat out:

Steak, Seafood, or Fast-Food Restaurant: Large dinner salad (salad entrées are increasingly popular) or salad bar; omelet; lean broiled meat or fish or chicken (with all visible fat trimmed off); boiled or steamed vegetables; plain scrambled or boiled eggs; most "diet plates," if they're truly low-calorie; cottage cheese or cottage-cheese salad; broiled chicken (no deep-fried stuff unless you peel off the skin and breading); tuna or chicken salad in a tomato or avocado half.

French restaurant: filet of sole; plain omelet or omelet *fines herbes;* mussels or fresh bluepoint oysters; plain grilled veal chop; bouillabaisse; poached sea bass, trout, or bay scallops; any salad with plain vinegar or lemon dressing, including salade Niçoise.

Greek restaurant: Greek salad (plain or village style, but skip the black olives and anchovies); gyros, roast lamb, shish kebab; egg-lemon soup; dolmades; spinach-cheese pie (leave the rich crust on the plate); Greek or Turkish coffee with no sugar (use artificial sweetener if you wish); plain yogurt.

Italian restaurant: Prosciutto and melon; vegetable plate (ask them to hold the sauce); a plain veal, chicken, or fish dish; scampi; veal paillard or chicken cacciatore; clams or mussels marinara. Pass up the desserts and have a cup of espresso with a twist of lemon peel instead.

Deli or coffee shop: Tuna or chicken salad plate (ask them to hold the mayonnaise or use low-fat substitutes); omelet or scrambled eggs; whole-wheat or pumpernickel bagel (no butter or cream cheese); tossed or mixed salad; roast beef, chicken, or turkey sandwich; side order of cottage cheese or hard-boiled eggs.

Some Final Words of Wisdom About Your Diet

1. Try varying the time and size of your meals. Who besides Mamma ever said you need three big square meals a day? Actually, the experts are right: 6 tiny snacks or minimeals are better than 3 big ones. The reason: your blood sugar level remains constant and you have none of the wild swings in mood and energy level, the headaches, nausea, or fatigue that we associate with dieting. But learn to think of a "meal" as 2 scoops of cottage cheese, a sliver of fruit, some vegetable sticks, and 2 ounces of water-packed chicken—not two vegetables in heavy sauce, a baked potato with sour cream, an 8-ounce steak, bread, butter, salad with Thousand Island dressing, and dessert. Also, try varying your eating pattern—you'll find it better to eat a larger breakfast and lunch (or brunch) and less at night. The same number of calories, ingested earlier in the day, tends to put on less weight than that huge meal at night. Breakfast, however hearty, is less likely to be stored as fat than the 8:00 P.M. steak dinner with all the trimmings.

2. Learn to recognize water-retention problems. Remember that plateaus in a diet, or even gains of a few pounds, can often be traced to fluid retention. Women usually have this problem at the start of the menstrual cycle, when they can pick up from 3 to 7 pounds of "free" water. Prescription diuretics, diuretic teas (cornsilk, rosehip, horsetail), noncarbonated, low-sodium mineral waters, and foods like asparagus and cucumber all help. Cut down on salt and all carbonated drinks that contain sodium and on foods that are naturally rich in sodium, like celery, if the problem continues.

3. So you want to be thin? Start practicing now! Start eating like a thin person instead of a fat one. Take small bites, nibble, don't gobble, and pause frequently between bites. Push the food around your plate and rearrange it before you begin to eat. Leave half of everything on your plate. Look around and pause again before you continue eating. And if you have a choice of restaurants, pick one with a view: sidewalk cafés and places with a street view are wonderful, since the people-watching can become so engrossing (for Valerie, at least) that food is forgotten.

   You can also learn to stretch a meal to 20, 30, even 40 minutes. Order a big salad as an entrée and eat it very slowly, one forkful at a time. You'll feel more satisfied with less food. It takes about 20 minutes for the "full" signal from the stomach and digestive tract to reach the brain. The slower you eat, the less it takes to satisfy you.

4. Try some "head tricks" of your own to keep yourself on the diet. Hang "before" and "after" pictures on your refrigerator door. Have a friend make "progress" snapshots of you as the pounds melt away. Buy one gorgeous thing that's just a size too small to inspire you to stay on the diet. And be sure to reward yourself at intervals: the 5-pound mark, the 10-pound mark, the 20-pound milestone. Just make sure the rewards aren't food related. No fair cheating!

5. Keep a diet diary. Get a small notebook and start writing down your weight and measurements at certain times (once a week at least) as well as everything you ate or drank each day. Include the amount, time, place, and circumstances under which you ate each bite. Figure up the total calorie count at the end of the day. It helps to know exactly how many calories you ate, and also when and why. If you know the times of day and the circumstances under which you overindulge, you can start correcting the patterns that lead to late-night refrigerator raids, party noshing, nibbling while you talk on the phone or watch television, or bedtime snacks.

6. Learn when weight-loss goals are realistic and when they're not. Back to our chapter on "Body and Soul." You may remember the *Glamour* magazine survey we cited, in which women revealed that many of them would prefer a 10-pound weight loss to success on the job or in love. It's all too easy to become obsessed with some "magic" number on the scales: what we weighed in college or the day we married, or before the first baby came.

If we've never been thin, we want to weigh what our best friend weighs or the latest model in the fashion magazines. What we often don't take into account is our individual bone structure and build. And don't dismiss all the latest research on set point theory. Have you ever noticed that when you're neither dieting strenuously nor pigging out every day your weight hovers around a certain figure week in and week out? That's your set point, and there's usually some rationale to the figure.

If you try to drop too suddenly or drastically under that figure, you may find yourself paying for it in terms of energy level, hair or skin quality, resistance to disease and cold, etc. The only way to lower the set point permanently, experts now believe, is through a long-term, systematic program of diet combined with exercise such as *Body-sculpture Plus* provides.

7. Finally, remember that the real battle isn't losing the weight but

keeping it off. We've already mentioned that of the millions of American women who lose weight each year, 90 percent regain the same amount, with interest, within a year. Don't look on your diet as something you go "on" and "off" but as a lifetime, ongoing process of learning to eat selectively, intelligently, and healthfully. The one way you'll assure yourself of never having to "go on" a diet again is to stay on a diet. You simply stay on a simple regimen of the right foods; then allow yourself an occasional splurge. The next day, back on the program you go! Just eat more of the right foods, less of the wrong ones, keep an eye on the scales, your tape measure, and the fit of your clothes as well. Sounds simple, but it works.

And best of all, it's good for you, makes you look smashing, feel great, and have energy to burn. And you'll *never* have to fight the Fat Demon again!

The *Bodysculpture Plus* Start-Up Diet

Note: this is a one-week diet to begin on Monday and continue through the following Sunday. You can repeat for as many weeks as you wish or switch to another calorie-controlled diet after the first week. Do not start on this or any other diet without first consulting your doctor.

Breakfast

- Hardboiled egg or 4 oz. cottage cheese (on alternate days)
OR
- 1 carton low-fat yogurt (plain or artificially flavored)
- 6 oz. grapefruit, low-sodium tomato, or low-sodium V-8 juice
- plain coffee or tea (no cream or sugar)

Lunch

- Large mixed green salad with dietetic dressing or plain vinegar (each day)
- 3 oz. cottage cheese or low-fat yogurt
- small apple, tangerine, wedge of melon, or 12 seedless grapes
- coffee, tea, or no-sodium diet soda

Dinner

- Broiled chicken or fish (4–5 oz) or one 6 oz. can water-packed chicken or tuna chunks
- Raw vegetable sticks with cottage cheese or yogurt dip
- 4 oz. steamed vegetables
- coffee, tea, or diet soda
- slice of melon or ½ tangerine, sectioned

Snacks

- Raw vegetables (any time); salt-free low-calorie soups, low-sodium vegetable juice, or unsweetened grapefruit juice; coffee, tea, and diet soda; whole-wheat crackers or rice cakes (60 calories' worth per day, eaten as desired)

Saturday and Sunday Brunch

- Omelet (plain or with farmer's cheese or other low-fat cheese, fresh vegetables or herbs)
- 1 "diet crêpe" (make with a base of 1 cup of cottage cheese, 1 egg, 2 packets of artificial sweetener, and a tablespoon of cornstarch for thickening); serve with fresh berries and a spoonful or 2 of a diet syrup
- Fresh melon wedge
- Perrier or Ramlosa water
- Espresso with a twist of lemon

Dinner

- Rock Cornish hen stuffed with chopped apple cubes, parsley, wedges of celery, seedless white grapes, and 4 tablespoons of brown rice mixed with bulgur wheat
- Asparagus tips steamed, with lemon juice dressing
- Mixed green salad
- Poached pear slices (poach in lemon juice, brandy extract, vanilla, cinnamon, and artificial sweetener)
- Espresso with a twist of lemon

THE NEXT STEP

The next step is to do something about the way you look while you're waiting for the bodyshaping programs and the diets to do their work. That's the subject of the next chapter, in which we show you all the tricks that will help you to look leaner in a hurry.

Chapter 8

All-New
Camouflage Fashions
for Work and Play

We've all indulged in those endless what-ifs that every dieter lives with: "What if I could only lose those last 10 pounds!" or "If only I could wear those (choose one): designer jeans/tight pants/slit skirts/skinny tank tops that everyone else is wearing this season . . ."

We all have this myth in our minds: that the diet and exercise routine we're on will make us wake up gorgeous one day. As we said in the first *Bodysculpture* book, it's the perfect fantasy. One day you'll walk into a party (or office, or restaurant, or convention, or whatever) and all eyes will turn to you. Everyone will drop his/her fork (glass/conversation/dining companion/cool/teeth/whatever) and murmur, "What a stunning woman just came into the room!"

Well, it does happen, of course. As a matter of fact, it now happens to Valerie all the time. But it doesn't always happen as quickly or as dramatically as we might wish. The changes take place slowly, sometimes maddeningly so. Meanwhile, our psychic state is already racing far ahead: our psyche is already lean and beautiful. It's the body that's lagging behind.

What to do? It's time for a short lesson on fashion as camouflage—a whole new theory of dressing and looking thinner than you are while those last 10 pounds come off.

Tricky? You bet it is! It's all visual sleight of hand aimed at making you look as if your routine were already an overwhelming success. And while the reality is catching up to you, you're already psyched up to stay with it until the last pounds come off simply because you look and feel so marvelous.

What is fashion as camouflage? It's the art of hiding those small figure flaws we all have—thick waist, short legs, heavy midriff, less-than-svelte ankles, chubby knees—and disguising them so that the viewer's attention is drawn to something else. Fashion as camouflage accentuates the good points and downplays any faults—and keeps you looking even better than you ever dreamed possible.

So first, some general rules of the game:

1. *For an overall slimmer look, try one-color dressing.* No, this needn't be a dull approach to fashion. There's nothing dull about a lean, strong, attractive woman in head-to-toe black: a simple black knit chemise or a black silk or crêpe dress, black pumps, dark-toned hose, simple but stunning silver jewelry, and hair tied back with a big black silk or velvet bow. Or for work, the same approach: a navy-blue or gray pinstripe or shadow-stripe suit, a toned-in silk blouse, the same stunning jewelry, shoes and hose toned in, one shade lighter or darker than the suit. It's an instant slimmer, regardless of your height or build—and a surefire way to look taller as well.

2. *Keep legs in the same color family as your outfit.* As we've mentioned above, toning in hose and shoes with the clothing gives that long, unbroken line we're after. Make sure that your boots meet the bottom of your skirt hem; nothing spoils the illusion like an inch or so of flesh-colored leg showing above the boot top!

3. *Use accessories to emphasize height and slimness.* Go for narrower, toned-in belts (hip belts are fine for the wide of waist), long flowing scarves or mufflers, shawls, long strands of pearls or beads, shoulder bags that swing from long chains or straps. Keep the vertical dimension as your point of emphasis and stay away from horizontal stripes, patterns, or anything that calls attention to width.

4. *In general, keep clothing soft, flowing, and loose-fitting.* No, we're not confining you to "big" looks, although handled correctly, they too can be slimming (more on this later). But your clothing should be made of material that moves and flows with you. Stiff, bulky fabrics tend to cling at all the wrong places. Soft knits, silks, supple jerseys, even thin suedes and leathers, and soft wools, including wool challis and thinner wool gabardines, are all good choices. Look for clothing that skims the body and doesn't cling or hug. An A-line skirt or one with soft, unstitched pleats is a better choice than the tight one that cups the fanny and clings to hips and thighs. Unless you're already pencil slim, leave those styles for your anorexic sisters.

5. *Don't forget to think of hairstyle and makeup while you plot your camouflage* (see the specific rules for "think thin" hairstyles and makeup at the end of the chapter). And remember that perfect grooming is an essential part of your camouflage. A well-cared-for woman radiates confidence and élan; a woman whose self-esteem is low doesn't care enough about herself to bother with hair, makeup, or nails. The instant you lose 5 pounds, reward yourself with a terrific new haircut, a makeup lesson, a good professional manicure. Each week try to spend at least one full hour working on your appearance: giving yourself a facial or pedicure, trying a hot-oil treatment for your hair, or weeding your wardrobe and shopping for new items. The "new you" deserves this extra pampering!

And now, on to our camouflage tips for those trouble spots:

For a Thick Waist

Where's the first place we usually notice a weight gain? Unfortunately, it's in the waist and midsection. But take heart: that's also one of the first spots to show weight loss! And while you're waiting for the endless crunches, side leans, and twists to take effect, here are some tips to get you started:

1. *Forget the standard advice: You don't have to forego belts just because you have acquired an extra inch here and there.* Just make sure your belt is toned into the outfit and is medium or thin in width. A basic luggage color is a good choice; so is burgundy, navy, charcoal gray, or black in widths from a half inch to an inch.
2. *Forget anything that cuts your figure in half or adds thickness or bulk to the waist.* The extra-wide new belts are fabulous for the small-waisted but a disaster on women with heavy middles. Ditto for dirndl and pleated skirts, unless the pleats are stitched or spaced; scarf-wrapped waists, bare midriff looks, or very short-waisted blouses or dresses with cinched waistlines. Forget the midriff-skimming sweaters and wide cummerbund-belted skirts and pants like the Perry Ellis collections for 1983 and 1984: wonderful for the lean but a disaster for the chubby. Also forget the wonderful scarf and belt-wrapped waists. They add extra bulk and call attention to the very area you're hiding.
3. *The trick is to draw attention from the natural (overweight) waist-*

line. Instead, try to create an artificial waistline by making a focal point elsewhere—just below the bust or at the hipbone. You can use "third layers" for this—a vest, a loose overblouse, a shirt or blouse worn like a jacket, a soft unlined jacket or cardigan sweater. Here you can use a narrow belt with an eye-catching buckle. Since the eye notices only the front of the belt, you get the polish and finish of the belt and also the length and vertical line of the top layering. Long sweater-vests in knits or thin fabrics are ideal. One instant slimmer is a sweater or blouse worn with classic pleated pants, a fabulous belt, a long classic knit sweater-vest, and a string of wooden, ivory, or silver beads. The long, simple lines subtract pounds and add inches, especially if you finish it off with a great pair of high-heeled pumps or sandals.

4. *Try some other waistline skimmers:* long, thigh-length blouses and sweaters, tunics, cardigans that skim the waistline or wrap loosely (like some of the classic Sonia Rykiels), slim overblouses, unbelted vests, ponchos or jackets. You can use a cape (provided it's graceful and moves well and is not made of stiff fabric) or even a long shawl or scarf or muffler that falls to the front and draws attention from the waistline. For evening, try a slim-cut chemise (they go in and out of fashion, but they are such classics, they always seem to work) or a long, lean tube style.

5. *Don't be afraid of dropped-waist dresses or chemises.* You do have to do some experimentation with these styles, but the newer dropped-waist dresses with long torsos and some hip interest (either as a hip wrap or some shirring or pleating at the hipline) are often wonderful looks for women with an extra inch or two at the waistline. If you see a style you like, by all means try it on. Not every style works for every woman, but unless it's too gimmicky or extreme, it may be right for you. And we repeat: don't forget the classic chemise. If it's slim-cut and hangs straight, particularly in a thin material and a dark shade, it can be a lifesaver for those last 5 stubborn pounds. Wear smashing jewelry and wait for the compliments to come in!

6. *Pick your belts with care.* As much as you might want them, pass over the superwide waist cinchers, the peasant braids, the wide metallic belts, braided and knit sashes, and all the other eye-catching paraphernalia until you've actually lost the pounds and inches. Simple leather belts (think Barry Kieselstein-Cord or one of the classier imitations) with an elegant silver or gold buckle are good choices, particularly a belt that's long enough to loop and knot. Collect striking buckles, especially interchangeable ones, since they draw atten-

tion to the center of the waistline and serve as instant pickups on otherwise monochromatic outfits.

7. *Don't feel that you always have to wear an unfitted top or overblouse.* Sometimes a top that's tucked in or worn on the outside, then belted over, is a more slimming look than an unbelted one. Another trick: try wearing a long tunic sweater or blouse over pants or a midcalf skirt, then belting it low on the hips with a special belt. It's a very contemporary look that still draws the eye away from the waistline.

8. *Don't be overly concerned about being long- or short-waisted.* You can always cheat a little by raising or lowering the natural waistline. But be careful about dropping the waistline too low if you're short: you can create the illusion of a woman with a very long torso and no legs at all! Remember to balance the silhouette you create.

9. *Sometimes a "waistline" problem turns out not to be a thick waist but a protruding tummy.* If that's the case with you, watch out for the clingy fabrics—and also for unpressed, unsewn pleats and gathers, or full dirndls. Also watch for the bulky-fabric skirts that accentuate the abdomen. You can wear graceful A-lines, even pleats (provided they're sewn down only four to five inches—not too far down the abdomen, please). You can also try eased wraps and modified dirndls (try one with gathers only at the sides and in the front). This is a wonderful style for nearly everyone, plump or thin, as is the inverted pleat in the center of a very slightly gathered A-line skirt. Many business suits now come with this type of skirt. And slash or side-seam pockets also give you a little extra fullness, and a place for your hands besides!

Heavy Hips and Thighs

Is there a woman anywhere who is really happy with the shape and size of her hips and thighs? We doubt it! Those two areas seem to be Everywoman's favorite trouble spot, and as a result, she's always looking for a new way to camouflage it. So here are our favorite tricks to downplay or hide hips and thighs until the *Bodysculpture Plus* program takes effect:

1. *Use pants for a slimming effect—but watch the cut!* It's become a kind of cliché that heavy women hide behind their stretch pants, which, ironically, often accentuate the very areas they should be hiding. The clingy polyester kind should definitely be avoided, but

on the other hand, there's no better camouflage for an extra pound or two than some easy-fitting, well-cut pants. You'll probably have to try on several pairs before you find the perfect ones, but almost everyone's best style is a pair of trouser-pleated, straight-falling, uncuffed pants that break over the shoe in exactly the right place. Avoid tapered, cropped, or flaring styles and seek out the classics for maximum wear and the most slimming effect. And avoid those tight polyester pull-ons in ice-cream colors at all costs!

One final note of caution: also avoid the jodhpurs, balloon and harem pants, the big baggies, and all the other fads of a few years past. They are fine for the slim of hip, but they'll show every extra bulge and roll! Stay on the *Bodysculpture Plus* routine and wear your classics with pride until the new shape emerges.

2. *Don't call attention to the hips with detail or decoration.* If you're bottom-heavy, your best rule is: keep it simple. That means no horse-shoe stitching on the back of your jeans, no decals or embroidery across your rear (and no designer labels either), no back pockets, no back gathers, no horizontal stripes emblazoned across your fanny. And no skintight *anything* unless you like to look as if you were poured into your clothes. Avoid any pants that you need a shoehorn to get into and any of the designer numbers that you have to lie on the floor to zip up!

As for shorts, take a good hard look at your rear in a three-way mirrow before you buy any. Do you really want to inflict that view on your fellow human-beings? Do them—and yourself—a favor and get some of the now chic loose-cut boxer shorts for women (very in with matching pastel tanks for gym and casual wear) and save the short-shorts for the days 10 pounds hence. For jeans, try the kind with a few eased pleats in front and a slim (not tight) back—Calvin Klein makes a good style of this kind. But please: no Charlie Chaplin baggies!

3. *If your rear is too heavy, cover it up!* You might call this the basic coward's way to camouflage, and perhaps it is. But it's also a safe, easy way to look 10 pounds lighter.

Remember those third layers we spoke of in the section on waists? Those same long jackets, tunics, pullover sweaters, long blouses, eased, unfitted jackets, and assorted shawls, capes, long scarves, and mufflers can be used to cover up heavy hips. Look for unfitted tops; the classic blazer is not a good choice for the bottom-heavy since it generally flares out wide over the heaviest portion of your anatomy. Besides, the classic styles often stop just short of the rear end, thus making you look even broader in the beam. John Molloy to the contrary, you'll look neater and more professional for work in a longer, unfitted jacket with some light shoulder padding to balance the silhouette.

4. *Don't feel you have to give up on skirts.* Instead, just choose the style wisely—one with pleats only in front, a classic A-line, a modified dirndl, a loose wrap, inverted pleat style, bias-cut and 4- to 6-gore knits and pull-ons are all good choices. Reject any styles that cup or cling at the rear or bulge over the tummy in front. And watch the heavy bulky fabrics again. Go with the lightweight, seasonless fabrics that move well without accentuating the area you'd just as soon forget.

5. *Finally, don't shy away from the oversized look or from layers.* Sounds contradictory, we know, but big-scale clothing or layers in thin fabrics aren't necessarily fat-making. As a matter of fact, an overscaled top, cape, or overblouse can be a lifesaver to the "hippy" figure, especially if she's well proportioned everywhere else. A few tips on layers, though: keep everything else small-scale and close to the body, except for one or two oversized pieces (a big tunic top, vest, cape, or overblouse is ideal). Let smaller pieces such as mufflers, belts or hip wraps, and jewelry carry the fashion message. Keep bottom layers (skirts and pants) simpler, with flat-weave fabrics and darker colors. And make sure that even the oversized pieces are in thin fabrics that move—no bulky tweeds for you. Instead, layer with thin (not thick) fleeces and sweatshirting fabrics, lightweight cottons and wools, flat knits.

And don't go for the total bag-lady look—oversized *everything*—especially if you're both short and heavy. Remember, proportion is the key. Try for a scaled-down version of the best designers of that layered Japanese look. Think Issey Miyake, Comme des Garçons, Yamomoto, and the look of funky elegance they convey—not Edna the Bag Lady.

Camouflage for Heavy Legs

At last we get to the area where Valerie is an expert! She spent the first 20-plus years of her life trying to hide her heavy calves and ankles—and the last 8 years trying to show off the proud results of her *Body-*

sculpture routine. But along the way, she's picked up some good ideas on camouflaging legs and ankles.

By the way, this is often a difficult area to camouflage, since shoes and boots are designed with the thin of leg in mind. If you believe the high-fashion glossies, no one, but no one, has this problem. There are two-page spreads full of exquisite gams in sensuous stockings and elegant shoes that would drive a foot fetishist mad. When some poor soul occasionally writes in for advice on what to do about fat calves, the harried fashion editor dashes off one line of advice: "Wear pants and cover them up!"

Fine. But what if you don't want to spend your life in pants? Or what if your office dress code—spoken or unspoken—dictates skirts and dresses instead? Then what?

Don't give up! Before you donate all of your dress-for-success skirted suits and elegant dresses to the Salvation Army, try these tips on leg camouflage and see what works best for you:

1. Back to our basic Rule One: *Maintain an unbroken line.* This is good, basic advice no matter what area you're trying to camouflage. Remember that whatever chops up a leg into different color areas shortens, thickens, and visually breaks the line of the leg. Result: your leg looks shorter and chunkier instead of longer and leaner.

   This means (alas!) that you'll have to choose legwear that's a bit on the conservative side. Don't be tempted by those wonderful, seductive ads of models in purple satin ankle boots, suede medieval-jester's wrap-and-tie numbers, or brilliant fuschia tights mixed with fur-trimmed leg warmers and wide satin garters. Those are wonderful fantasy costumes, but not for you.

   If your legs are less than pencil slim, your best bet is to coordinate both shoes and hose to your skirt, not your top. For example, a skirt in black or navy requires either black/navy shoes and hose, or boots in a darker color, that hit the shirt hem (perferably some that extend beyond it). No gaps, ever!

   The color range for you is dark: black, deep charcoal gray, maroon, wine, dark brown, navy blue, even offbeat darks like burgundy and deep hunter green. Remember that toning is the key: the colors don't have to match exactly, but they should be shades or tones of one another. Dark brown semisheer hose and dark brown pumps with a chocolate-colored skirt, black or deep charcoal with a pewter-colored or black dress, deep maroon hose and burgundy pumps with a burgundy silk dress—you get the picture?

   The formula we've invented here need not be dull. The shoes can he two-toned. In fact, the classic Chanel pump in a light color and a dark toe can be wonderful for women with heavy legs. Fashionable dark-colored boots are perfect. The skirt can vary in style, material, and cut. Even the hose can have a subtle rib or tiny overall pattern. But again, toning-in is the key. The same tone or shade of the same color creates that long unbroken line we're after.

2. *Don't shy away from light tones:* just apply the formula. White, beige, and ivory are wonderful, classic, rich-looking colors, but often women with heavy legs feel that they are forbidden to them. If you've been falling into that trap, go and pull out the white skirt from the back of your closet. Try it with a slightly darker shade of sheer hose (perhaps a light suntan shade) and tone in with a simple pump or sandal in beige, pale, off-white (stark white can accentuate heavy legs). But *don't* fall for the white-hose fad that has been making the rounds for several years now. It can make heavy legs look 5 pounds heavier. Go for pale gray or another pastel tone instead.

   Even if your dress-for-success manual dictates natural-colored hose for the office, a darker suntan shade is better than a flesh tone. Even the most conservative office will never notice the difference, and the darker tone is infinitely more flattering to your legs. L'Eggs Sheer Energy in coffee is a good tone to try; it's a light support hose that prevents swelling and is flattering to most skin tones.

3. *Don't rely on opaque stockings to solve your leg problems.* The really opaque stockings that we see so much of nowadays are sometimes poor choices for heavy legs. They often look hot and add inches, particularly in warm weather. They wrinkle and bag easily, and can give you a sort of stodgy, matronly look if you're not careful. A semiopaque in a dark tone is a better choice. And no matter how great the temptation, stay away from the brilliant reds and blues that fashion has fallen in love with. They're so eye-catching that they call attention to your legs and nothing else.

   The exception to our "no heavy opaques" rule? Whenever you're wearing boots. Valerie always wears dark opaque tights with her boots (she has them in navy, black, and dark brown leather and charcoal gray patent) since they give waist-to-toe coverage. Even if she's seated and the boot top is visible, there's a nice dark shade of hose showing instead of bare leg.

4. *A list of don'ts: avoid ankle straps, mary janes, short ankle-length boots, short socks, kooky patterned hose, lace-trimmed anklets, lace-up shoes and ankle-ties, Oxfords.*

   Sorry, but there are some things you have to forego forever if your legs are heavy. We've already suggested the best DO: a wide-throated, high-vamp shoe, preferably a pump, in a dark color. A medium-high to high slender, straight, tapered or cone-shaped heel is best. Try the new higher cone-shaped heels; for some reason they work very well.

Beware the retro-looking spool heels and the needle-thin stiletto heels. They can make your leg look as if it was so heavy it crushed the heel down by its sheer weight. Inward-curving or "shaped" heels just don't work for heavy-legged women.

On the other hand, you're not consigned to the plain dark pump forever. While it's flattering and appropriate with most clothing, it can get boring—so vary it with simple sandals (no ankle straps unless you're wearing pants or evening pajamas); low-cut T-straps, Chanel-style slingbacks, high, narrow wedge heels, even lace-ups and ghillies if they're worn with pants. Medium-thick platforms (no Minnie Mouse looks, please) are fine because they give some coun-terbalancing weight to the foot and also add height.

And when in doubt, try on. Even a shoe that defies all the rules may work for you. Valerie once fell in love with some ankle-wrap Carrano sandals in a light luggage color, and although they violated all of her self-made rules, she simply had to have them. For some reason they worked for her, despite the ankle ties—maybe because of the neutral color and the thin platform soles. At any rate, five years later, they're still in her wardrobe and they taught her a valuable lesson. Rules still exist to be broken, and *you* have to be the judge of what looks good on you.

5. *Wear boots, boots, boots!* Just make sure the style works with your outfit and that they're tall enough to meet your skirt.

Boots are truly a godsend for women with heavy legs—provided they fit. Unfortunately, many of the zip-up styles are cut too small for women with really heavy legs. But when you've done your *Bodysculpture Plus* routines faithfully, you'll find you can wear most pull-on styles and even some zips, with ease.

Your best boot bets are knee-high or longer. The coachman's boot with flip-back cuffs is wonderful. So are the thigh-high pull-on rain boots that are now so popular; they're good choices for rainy days when you need to keep dry and look neat when you arrive at your office or appointment. You can also wear such innovative styles as the crushed or slouch boot, high-fashion knock-offs of the cowboy or Western boot (like Valerie's gray patent Walter Steigers), and so on. Just make sure they all have a heel; flat boots tend to shorten and thicken the calf, at least visually.

In general, stay away from short (ankle-length or mid-calf) boots unless you plan to wear them only with pants. The leg showing between boot top and skirt or dress is not flattering. High heels are better than flats; even if you can't or don't wear skyscraper heels, you need a little lift—a stacked or tapered heel of even an inch or two will help you carry off a slimmer look.

6. *Use stockings with caution.* Styles like lace tights, wild prints, geometrics, and other large patterns are fine with pants but not with skirts. For wear under pants, anything goes: the red lace anklets, the wildly patterned Perry Ellis tights, the geometrics in hot colors (they're wonderful as a hit of color that shows only when you cross your legs). But with skirts, the same amusing and colorful hose are a disaster. They'll just call attention to your heavy legs.

   And contrary to some "expert" advice, all-over vertical stripes and ribbing can make heavy legs look even heavier. The pattern in the stripes runs askew, especially if both knees and calves are heavy, and the look is never neat. If your calves are thin, go ahead. But over really chunky calves, a tiny overall pattern such as a herringbone or a tiny pin dot or diamond design is a better choice.

7. *Wear pants—but make sure they don't cling to the leg.* Like boots, your pants are a godsend, but only if they're the right look. Go for the classic, tailored style—no back pockets (side or slash pockets in front are fine), no cuffs. But *never* tight, especially over the calf. Some of the more fashionable and innovative styles that are around now are too calf-hugging—the revived fifties clam-diggers, toreadors, jodhpurs, etc.—and simply don't work on anyone with calves that are not pencil thin. Stay with your classics and look for innovations in fabric and color instead of style.

8. *Do try "divided skirts" or culottes—*but only if they fit loosely and move well. These pants/skirt hybrids have been in and out of fashion for years, it seems—and women with heavy legs can wear only certain versions of them. The best divided skirts are loosely cut, softly-pleated styles that fall easily from the waist. Try them loose (not big, but not clinging either) with dark-toned shoes and hose or boots. The black silk ones for evening can be mid-calf or ankle-length. They're elegant camouflage, as are evening pajamas. Add a glittery top and go dancing!

9. *Try wearing long skirts and pants for evening wear.* If your main problem is heavy legs run, do not walk, to your favorite store or boutique and invest in two items: an ankle-length black skirt (silk or a thinner fabric is generally better and more graceful than velvet, unless it is a very thin velvet or wool); and a pair of black silk

evening pajamas—no elephant legs, but no tight pants either. With these two items, plus an array of colorful tops, you could travel around the world and still be well dressed for anything, except possibly a royal wedding. Both items hide your legs, are versatile, mix easily, adapt to any climate, and look terrific year in and year out.

10. *If you can possibly do it, wear high heels with pants.* Unless you have a foot problem that is so bad you just can't wear high heels at all, do experiment with wearing a higher heel with pants. It's a more elegant look that makes women appear less dumpy and squat, whether they are heavy or average-sized. The extra height can make the difference between looking short and dumpy or tall and lean. Classic high-heeled pumps with tailored pants are a stylish, contemporary look that can go from office to dinner after work and still look both polished and professional.

For a Heavy Upper Body

Although most women's weight is concentrated toward the lower half of their bodies (the pear-shaped people), there are also the ice-cream-cone shapes with the weight concentrated near the top. If you're heavy on top, you may be too heavy in the arms (especially the upper arms), the back and shoulders, or the bust area. So here's a short primer to help you camouflage your problem spots just as your bottom-heavy sisters do.

For Flabby Upper Arms

First, a cheerful note. Flabby upper arms, like a flabby waistline, are among the first areas to respond to training. So your camouflage may end up being short-lived indeed! But while you're waiting out the arms routine, here are a few tips to consider:

1. *Avoid strapless and backless styles, sleeveless dresses and tops, halters, spaghetti straps, muscle-sleeved tops, and other short or bare styles.* If you have heavy arms you'll have to forego all the bare-is-

beautiful sexy styles in the stores (sigh). The one exception: if you have items like this left from slimmer days, try wearing them under a short evening cape or shawl that gives the look of bareness in front and cover the arms at the same time.

2. *Try bell and scarf-type sleeves, long, ¾, and elbow-length sleeves.* No reason to be dull about it! You can wear sleeves of many lengths and sizes. The important thing is to keep the arms covered. Even small cap sleeves in summer are more flattering than a bare arm, and just as cool.

As you begin to lose pounds and inches, you may find that a halter-style top is more flattering than a sleeveless one—perhaps because it bares more shoulder and so gives more illusion of length to the arm. Look for a halter-neck maillot or bikini for beach wear for maximum arm flattery.

For Heavy Back, Shoulders, and Neck

1. *For wide or heavy shoulders, avoid cap or dolman sleeves.* Also avoid the exaggerated wedge shape and the padded shoulder that can be so flattering to hip-heavy women. You'll want to keep the line at the shoulder simple and close to the body. Try shoulder seams that lie one inch inside the real shoulder line to achieve a narrower look on top. And no pleats or puffs or puckering at the sleeves, please!

2. *Avoid heavy or bold horizontal patterns or squared necks, yokes, and bateau necklines.* Plain silk blouses with very gentle gathering or plain shoulders are a better style. And generally, raglan sleeves are better than boxy, square-cut sleeves. Square sleeves are in at the moment, but times will change. Be patient!

3. *If your neck is both thick and short, stay away from turtlenecks and cowls.* Even classic crew necks may be wrong for you. Instead, go for slimming V-necks and low, scooped-out classic round necks. Unless your shoulders are also heavy, bateau, or "boat," necks are also okay.

4. *Even if your neck is thicker than you'd like, you don't have to eschew high fashion forever.* Sometimes exaggerated Vs or low cowls, front or back, are flattering to women with heavy necks. Exaggerate the vertical dimension with long strands of beads or pearls, elongating scarves, or long mufflers in thin fabrics. A long silk muffler, knotted low on the neck, is a pounds-off trick for everyone. Be imaginative!

For a Heavy Bust

If your problem is a "busty" look, you can go in either of two directions: you can flaunt your assets or hide them. The problem usually isn't bust size but proportion: a woman with a large bust and a small waist is a traffic stopper in anyone's book. But a woman who is heavy all over and has a large bust (*and* waist *and* hips *and* thighs) is just *fat*. If that's your problem, follow these tips:

1. *Avoid anything that accentuates the problem area.* And that includes Empire waistlines or anything else that is tucked or gathered under the bust. Also skip the tailored shirts tucked into skirts (especially if the shirt is buttoned up tight at the neck), chemises (unless they flare at the hemline), skinny-rib tight sweaters or polo shirts, the no-bra look, suspenders, peasant-style or puffed-sleeve blouses, wide horizontally-striped tops, and huge ruffled necklines. And leave the multitucked, lacy Victorian whites to your small-busted sisters. They're beautiful vintage fashion and very high style, but you'll end up looking like a Gibson Girl reject.
2. *Do use loose fit and elongated lines to deemphasize the bust area.* Your best bets are deep V-necks, loose button-front blazers or jackets (avoid double-breasted ANYTHING like the plague), draped or shirred bodices, unfitted overblouses (also open cardigans or vests)—in short, anything that skims the body and doesn't fit tightly. Loose, unfitted, "unconstructed" blazers or jackets are a better choice than the fitted blazer, which tends to be snug across the bust. Also, try hip belts or a hip wrap with pants or skirts. That way, you move the natural waistline down a bit and hence the focal point of your outfit is lower.
3. *Do use well-constructed bras to get the support you need.* Save the no-bra look for your small friends (who are probably wishing they had your problem). And never, never, ever try to run or do aerobics braless. The constant pounding motion can break down delicate breast tissue and cause permanent sag. Try a good sports bra under your leotard or T-shirt.
4. *Avoid looking as if you were stuffed into your clothes.* The worst thing in the world is a heavy woman squeezed into a top a size or two too small. Acknowledge your real size and wear it. Spend money on alterations if necessary. Set-in armholes can help, but they must be

well fitted. And don't let clothes look as if they're hanging on you, either. Make sure they are well fitted even if they're loose bell or boxy-style sleeves.

Some General Tips on Camouflage

Often when we think of camouflaging figure faults, we think of specific items—a blazer, a skirt, a jacket—never stopping to remember that it's the overall look that's important. Every piece counts, from your overcoat or raincoat to your shoes. So here are a few general wrap-up rules that can mean the difference between looking 10 pounds heavier or lighter than you are:

1. *For outerwear, think simple and classic.* Avoid huge cloaks or capes (unless they drape softly, preferably asymmetrically). They can make you look like an elf hiding under a toadstool. Skip the long-haired furs, especially if they are horizontally worked, and wear short jackets with caution. The popular fur "chubby" is not for you. Seven-eighths or mid-calf length is a better choice. Instead try a vertically worked, short-haired fur with a simple cut in a dark color.

   For your everyday wool coat or raincoat, go for a simple updated classic: a pea coat, trench, or reefer is a good choice. Pick a wrap style with caution; you need to try on several styles before you make a choice. Make sure the material is not too bulky to fall well. Now that wider shoulders are popular, you might consider a flanged or pleated-shoulder style that falls straight and unbelted. In a brilliant red or cobalt blue these coats look avant-garde; in charcoal gray, camel, or black, they're Wall Street conservative. The shoulder width draws attention from your waistline and hips and gives you more mass where most women need it. And the unbelted style is simple and flattering to nearly everybody.

2. *Other things to avoid, across the board: very narrow, pencil-slim skirts* (we know: they come and go in fashion, but save them for the time you reach your weight-loss goal). Also avoid wide collars, big cartwheel hats of the garden-party variety (great for the slim but not so for the heavy, unless you're very tall), horizontal stripes, capes worn with short skirts (wrong proportion—try them with long or calf-length skirts), flat heels (you need a little lift), short, stiff peplums or tight bustiers, giant prints, and any shiny, stiff fabrics, such as satins.

3. *Hair length is also important.* No look is going to work for you unless you also take the lines of your hair into consideration. And there's no one style that works for everyone. In general, very long straight hair is a disaster on heavy women, regardless of age—and it's especially aging and dowdy-looking on heavy women past 25. If you must keep your hair long, tie or pin it back for business and everyday wear.

Some styles to consider if you're heavy: a basic blunt cut (anywhere from chin-length to collarbone-length), depending on your individual facial structure; a tapered or layered medium-length cut (good for thick hair with plenty of body); even a tapered short cut, provided it's not too severe—you need some hair on top to keep the head from getting "lost" above the body mass. As you begin to lose weight, experiment with small, close-to-the-head styles such as small chignons or buns for evening (you can tie them or lace them with narrow ribbons or bits of metallic cord or silk flowers). The small-head "do" will emphasize your new small proportions as you lose weight.

4. *The one thing to avoid with hair styles is an elaborate, over-contrived look.* We said in the original *Bodysculpture,* and we'll say it again: the fat-lady look, with tons of pancake makeup and teased curls is one recognizable cliché that we all know. Don't fall for it. A simpler, more natural hairstyle looks both thinner and younger. If your hair is naturally curly, go for a controlled, neatly styled curly look that can be distinctive and dramatic, not just messy.

5. *Think of hats, scarves, and other accessories as part of the total outfit.* Keep lines close to the body. Simple, small knit caps, soft felt or straw fedoras, crushable brimmed rainhats, silk or cotton headwraps and scarves are good choices for you. If you adore big hats, as Valerie does, and you can find one in the color and style you want, go for it—but remember to keep the size in proportion to your own. Valerie secretly craves the garden-party styles but finds they overwhelm her small frame, so she compromises with smaller-scaled boaters and fedoras with low crowns.

6. *While we're on the subject of accessories, you'll want to rethink yours with a critical eye.* Edit out the huge oversized bags, the itsy-bitsy cute purses, the tight dog collars or chokers, jeweled harlequin glasses (unless you're into a total Retro look), giant pussycat bows, or high-buttoned collars—anything that accentuates the horizontal dimension. Substitute long scarves or mufflers in silk or other thin fabrics, shoulder bags hanging from long straps, long chains or pearls, long, thin envelope bags. Go for drop earrings—a better

choice than round buttons—or for strong elongated geometric shapes. Belts should have a strong center focal point, such as one of the striking Peretti silver buckles, to draw attention to the center of the waist and away from the sides. Make sure the belt is dark colored, however.

7. *Start building a wardrobe of shoes to flatter and lengthen your legs visually while you continue with the* Bodysculpture Plus *leg routine.* Slingbacks, high-heeled pumps, wide-throated sandals and wide-throated moccasins, plus plenty of fashionable boots, will all work for you. Skip the flat-as-a-pancake heel and go for a small heel, at least two inches or more. If you start your shoe wardrobe with high-heeled dark pumps to wear with both skirts and pants, add wide-throated sandals for summer and boots for winter, you can gradually expand from that point.

Thinking/Acting/Being Lean

Want some head tricks to make yourself look and feel leaner than you are even while you still have some pounds to lose? Try these on for size—one size smaller than you are!

First, remember to think of your posture and overall carriage as ways to look slimmer. They're part of your camouflage, too. Practice walking tall with graceful, easy strides (think of Lady Julia Marchmain walking her golden retrievers through the fields at Brideshead on an autumn evening to get in the proper mood). Or think of yourself 20 pounds lighter, striding down (pick one) the Champs Elysée/the Via Veneto/Fifth Avenue/the Magnificent Mile on your way to buy something wonderful in a size 6!

Remember a trick that professional models have known and used for a long time: don't face your audience—or the camera—head-on if you can turn a slight angle. The trick is to stand with one hip angled out ever so slightly, one foot just in front of the other. Don't do an exaggerated "model's pose"—just don't stand with your feet together.

Same trick when sitting: don't sit with your two fat knees together or crossed exactly at the knee (makes all the fat bulges reappear). Instead, put your feet together and angle the knees to the side—or cross the legs high on the thigh. Or sit with one foot behind the other. Study graceful women, in life and in photographs, for tips. You don't want to become hyperconscious of all this so that you can't stand or sit without thinking of the way your legs are crossed, but you *can* develop naturally graceful and slimming ways of moving, sitting, and standing that make you look better to everyone.

Think lean! In the "Body and Soul" chapter, we've already talked about the need to let your body image keep up with your actual weight loss as well as the need *not* to let yourself get into the trap of being dominated by a "magic number" on the scales.

Now let's talk about another aspect of thinking lean. There's a fat mind-set and a lean one, as we said earlier. The fat soul falls into a rut of not caring how her body looks. She clumps up steps, waddles down the street, flops into chairs, heaves herself off and onto buses, and into taxicabs. She doesn't perceive herself as a vital or sensual human being, and you can tell it from everything she does. Her body language gives her away. When she eats in a restaurant, she's feeding her face, not dining. When she's talking with friends, she isn't conscious of her gestures or movements.

The person with a lean mind-set, by contrast, is always conscious of her body. No, we don't mean self-conscious, shy, or embarrassed, just conscious. The woman with the lean mind-set walks lightly and quickly, with long strides, down the street. She sits easily and gracefully. In a restaurant, she's doing more than feeding her face; she's also looking around, pausing, talking, watching other people, aware of her environment. She is aware of how she's standing at the bus stop or in line. She is actively climbing onto that bus or into the cab, not just throwing herself and her briefcase/bag/coat/parcels/whatever/ into it. A subtle difference, but one that any dedicated people-watcher will pick up right away. The body language is instant, and it communicates a message very precisely.

The cure for the fat mind-set? Allow your mental image to keep pace with your physical one. One of the many pluses of slow weight loss is that it allows your mental image to readjust along with your physical self. Begin by forming a mental image of yourself as a lean person. Pull out an old photo of yourself at your ideal weight (even if it's in high school or college days). If you've always been heavy, take a recent photo and "trim away" the fat with scissors to get an idea of what you will look like 20, 30, 40, pounds lighter. Hang both the original and the "doctored" version on the refrigerator door.

Now start thinking ahead to where you will be in three to six months. Imagine yourself without the extra pounds. Since this is fantasy, you can make yourself as lean as you wish to be. While you're at it, gain—or lose—a couple of inches in height. Get the ideal shape you've always wanted.

And now: start moving, walking, standing as if you were that person in your fantasy. Imagine what you would wear and how you would act and move. There may be special clothes that help you keep the image in your head; if so, wear them often to remind yourself of the changes that are taking place in you. Do all of your motions each day with this imaginary person (yourself in six months?) in mind. And you'll find yourself actually growing more like the image in your head.

Become fashion-conscious. No, we don't mean that you should become a slave to "in" and "out" (although that can be fun at times) or that you should become vain and excessively preoccupied with yourself. But as you develop that healthy sense of self-esteem and of living inside a body you like and enjoy, you will want to know some new and different ways to dress and make up.

You see, fat women tend to become fashion dropouts. Valerie was for years. Fat women dig through racks of sizes 4 and 6, trying in vain to spot a larger size, listen to ads for smaller-than-small and thin-is-in boutiques, read all the fashion hype for the pencil-slim look—even watch skinny mannequins touting health clubs and exercise studios, and hear lean, svelte celebrities extolling their latest exercise books. And the fat women start tuning out all that thin hype, even the best of it, and turn to their comfortable stretch pants and tried-and-true tent dresses.

Try to change all that as you begin to drop the pounds. No, we're not recommending that you become vain or obsessed with your wardrobe. But we *are* recommending that you become aware of fashion and the way it can aid you in looking and feeling better about yourself.

So while you're on the *Bodysculpture* routine, sharpen your eye for fashion and your sense of proportion. Window-shop. Brave those oh-so-chic little boutiques and fashionable department stores that you were afraid to enter before. Take a friend along for moral support and try on something outrageous. Or just browse to get a sense of new styles, colors, proportions.

Remember that it doesn't cost anything to look! Read catalogs and fashion magazines. People-watch. Devote an entire afternoon to window-shopping and people-watching as you sip your mineral water or iced tea. Weed out your wardrobe and give away your "fat" clothes to your favorite church or charity. As you replace the tents and the stretch pants, make sure you replace them with quality clothes that fit perfectly to flatter your new shape.

Don't forget that the right makeup can resculpt your face just as exercise reshapes your body. You probably will find that your weight loss shows in your face even before it shows in the rest of you. Now is the time to invest in a good professional makeup (preferably one with a lesson plan or instructions so you can learn to do the magic for yourself). Learn the art of highlighting newly defined cheekbones, creating cheek hollows, contouring an overly round or square face into a perfect oval. Play up your eyes and lips with new makeup techniques. If your makeup is perfectly and artfully done, no one will notice that you still have 5 pounds left to lose.

And while you're at it, start building a good basic wardrobe. In the original *Bodysculpture*, we recommended a Basic Four-Part Camouflage Wardrobe. It's still as basic and necessary as ever: pants, skirt, blouse, and jacket. Since you're trying to build a wardrobe virtually from scratch, in a new smaller size, make all the pieces in a single color or shades thereof. A dark or neutral color that is suitable for business is your best choice: navy, gray, camel, black, dark chocolate brown, a deep burgundy, or hunter green, if you can afford to be a little more daring in the office.

You might want to make the blouse a contrasting color—wine or claret for a navy or black suit; cream or ivory for a gray outfit, etc. Make sure your fabric is lightweight and seasonless; we recommend a lightweight wool gabardine, wool crêpe, or thin knit fabric than can span the seasons. In winter, you can add sweaters for warmth; in summer, light cotton T-shirts and polo shirts, or bright linen and cotton blouses and jackets can add variety.

Make sure the lines of the outfit provide good camouflage. The blouse can be a softly tailored style (perhaps with a self-tie or bow at the neck); a softly flared A-line skirt, classic slim-cut pants, and a long unfitted (fanny-covering) jacket or blazer. Add accessories and you're ready for anything. This is a wardrobe you can build on from year to year. At first you may have nothing else except a classic raincoat or overcoat, a thin dark or neutral-colored belt, some good jewelry (thin gold and silver chains, pearls and classic earrings are good basics), some silk scarves and an elegant shawl for evening, good leather shoes and a pair of boots, and a classic leather briefcase and bag. That's enough to keep you looking chic and businesslike as you start that new life as a thin person.

The beauty of this four-part wardrobe is that you can add to it year by year. Next season, spring for an extra cardigan, vest or sweater, and another silk blouse, another skirt, an extra pair of pants. The following summer's buys are a linen skirt, some linen or cotton blouses, and another unfitted jacket. Next fall: a pair of black silk evening pants and a cashmere sweater. And so on. You can always add to the wardrobe by shopping sales, resale and thrift shops, and rummage sales where you can pick up inexpensive tops and accessories to vary and update your look. And before you know it, you'll have collected the perfect wardrobe for the new you—just what you need to hide your problem spots, flaunt your strong points, and generally show off the results of those months of hard work.

Happy shopping—and happy camouflage, everyone!

Afterword: And So Can You

So now you've come to the end of *Bodysculpture Plus*. You have read the updated version of Valerie's famous fight with the Fat Demon. You've learned how to psych yourself up and keep yourself motivated to continue the *Bodysculpture* program. You've learned what equipment to buy and how to tell a good health club from the scams. You've also learned what exercises to do for bodysculpting, for aerobic training, and for gains in suppleness, grace, and flexibility.

More important, you've learned how to combine all those exercises into programs that work for each one of you, individually, regardless of your problems, your schedule, or your special trouble spots. Finally, you've learned about diet and nutrition and about using fashion to camouflage those special trouble spots until the *Bodysculpture Plus* program takes effect.

So good-bye to you, to all our readers who've followed us from *Bodysculpture* to this new program and new book. We've enjoyed our chance to talk with you personally, in small groups, or individually, and to answer your questions by letter or by radio or television. We hope you'll stay in touch and let us know about your progress.

We know you'll do it. Valerie did. And so can you. Remember that you are the only thing standing in the way of having the body shape you've always wanted. It just takes your weights, a good diet, this book, and a lot of determination.

So good luck and Godspeed. We're on your side, and we're behind you all the way!

Index to the Resistance Exercises, Chapter 5

Index

199